ALLIANCE guide to
TAX & YOUR HOME

ALLIANCE guide to
TAX & YOUR
HOME

W. D. ROTHENBERG M.A, FCA

BLICK ROTHENBERG & NOBLE

Abbreviations

CGT	capital gains tax
CGTA	Capital Gains Tax Act 1979
CTT	capital transfer tax
DLT	development land tax
DLTA	Development Land Tax Act 1976
ESC	Extra-Statutory Concession
FA	Finance Act
GRA	General Rate Act 1967
ICTA	Income and Corporation Taxes Act 1970
IR11	Inland Revenue booklet, *Tax Treatment of Interest Paid*
IR20	Inland Revenue booklet, *Residents and Non-Residents Liability to Tax in the United Kingdom*
IR25	Inland Revenue booklet, *The Taxation of Foreign Earnings and Foreign Pensions: Finance Act 1977*
LGA	Local Government Act 1972
MIRAS	mortgage interest relief at source
para.	paragraph
PR	Inland Revenue Press Release
RA	Rating Act 1971
s.	section
SA	Stamp Act 1891
sch.	schedule
SI	Statutory Instrument
SP	Inland Revenue Statement of Practice
TMA	Taxes Management Act 1970

First published in Great Britain 1984 by Financial Training Publications Limited, Avenue House, 131 Holland Park Avenue, London W11 4UT

© W. D. Rothenberg, 1984

ISBN: 0 906322 63 4

Typeset by Kerrypress Ltd, Luton
Printed in Great Britain by Redwood Burn Ltd, Trowbridge

Foreword

Since the beginning of civilised society taxation has been the principal means by which governments have raised money from the people and no one has yet come up with a better way of raising funds for public expenditure.

The tax system in this country is both complex and multifarious, and the more complex our lives become the more difficult it is to keep abreast with the changing regulations which govern our financial affairs.

Home owners in this country enjoy special taxation privileges. They can acquire a major capital investment on a long-term loan, the interest on the first £30,000 of which is tax deductible, and they pay no tax on the capital gain.

These privileges are not a quirk of fate, successive governments — particularly the present one — have been keen to encourage home ownership, and the enormous growth of building societies since the second world war has made it possible for the majority of the people to raise the funds to buy their own homes. Over 60% of our homes are now owner-occupied and this figure is still growing. A recent survey showed that most young people these days expect to own their own homes.

Buying or selling a house is probably the largest financial transaction that most of us will conduct in our lifetime. It is a complex procedure and one on which taxation has a major influence.

How many of us have the proper training or the knowledge to understand fully the relationship between home ownership and taxation?

In this excellent book, David Rothenberg, a specialist in the subject, looks at every aspect of taxation and how it affects or is affected by our status as home owners. Whether we own one or more homes, buy it or have it given to us, rent it or occupy it as part of an employment contract, this book explains every aspect of the taxation equation and how we can properly manage our affairs to our best advantage.

I like especially the way in which David Rothenberg explains complex financial procedures and jargon in simple everyday language, using many examples to clarify the more complicated transactions. The further advice service, unique to this book, offered to readers will be of particular value to those with specific queries.

Occasionally a textbook is written which can be referred to equally well by the expert and the layman. This is one of them, and I thoroughly recommend it to everyone who owns a home, is thinking of owning one, or has anything to do with the subject.

Roy Cox
Chief Executive
The Alliance Building Society

Preface

The largest financial transaction most of us undertake in our lives is the acquisition of our homes. The tax system has been adapted, eased and changed over the years to reflect this fact.

Whether you are a home owner or hope to become one, rent your home or occupy it rent-free, this book has been written to answer your questions and perhaps to bring to your attention some problems of which you may not have been previously aware. It covers all those occasions when the tax system and your home interact.

The final chapter of the book contains some of the questions people ask on how their tax may be affected by their homes and what they do with them, and suggests answers to those questions based on what is said in the previous chapters.

It is hoped that the book may also be of use to solicitors, estate agents, bank managers and others who are asked by their clients to help answer some of these questions.

Particular emphasis has been placed on the problems which might arise if you work abroad for a time, as this, nowadays, is a part of many people's experience.

The book inevitably simplifies some of the more complex areas of law — it is a guide and not a legal textbook. If you cannot find the answer to your questions you should consult a specialist in the field, whether an accountant, a solicitor or a qualified surveyor.

The book is based on the law as at 6 August 1984, including the Finance Act 1984 and the Capital Transfer Tax Act 1984.

In writing this book I should like to express my thanks to Tim Myers of the Alliance Building Society, to John Gibbs and Alistair MacQueen of Financial Training Publications Ltd and to my colleague, Alfred Homburger, FCA, BCom, ACMA, who have nurtured the project from its inception; to Robert Jamieson, MA, FCA, FTII, of Financial Training (Specialist Courses) Ltd and to my colleague, John Newman, BA, FCA, who have read the manuscript and made invaluable comments; to Robert Rothenberg, BA, FCA, ATII, who formulated the problems in Chapter 18; to Flora Jumeau who typed the manuscript; to Heather Saward for her calm guidance and, above all, to my wife, Ruth, who revised, rewrote and typed the drafts and without whose support this book would not have happened.

David Rothenberg
London, September 1984

Contents

1 An outline of the United Kingdom taxation system

'It was as true,' said Mr Barkis, '. . . as taxes is. And nothing's truer than them.'

David Copperfield, Charles Dickens

That statement is just as true today! Almost whatever we do, wherever we go and whatever activity we undertake, one or more taxes will affect us. How your home will affect those taxes is explained in the succeeding chapters. The basic questions in connection with the tax system are: Who? What? When? And how much?

There are various different taxes which are paid in the United Kingdom; the ones with which this book is concerned are only the taxes which are, or may be, affected by your home. They are income tax, capital gains tax (CGT), capital transfer tax (CTT), development land tax (DLT), stamp duty, value added tax (VAT) and rates. A simple outline of the income tax and capital gains tax systems is set out in this chapter.

1.1 Who has to pay taxes?

In this book taxes payable to the United Kingdom government or local authorities are considered. Taxes are collected from (a) individuals, (b) companies, (c) societies, clubs and associations, and (d) people who hold assets on behalf of others such as executors or trustees. Since neither companies nor clubs and associations will occupy homes, the special tax rules concerned with corporation tax and which apply to companies (and also to clubs and associations) are not within the scope of this book at all.

1.2   Individuals

The term 'persons' is a broad term which in law covers not only individuals but also 'bodies corporate', more usually known as companies. In order to distinguish ordinary people, the term 'individuals' is applied to them. In tax law you are an individual. You may be subject to United Kingdom taxes if you are resident (see Chapter 12), or ordinarily resident, in the UK or alternatively, even if you are not physically in the UK at all, if you have assets or sources of income which are located within the UK. If you are neither resident in the UK nor have any assets or sources of income in the UK, you might still be subject to UK capital transfer tax if you are still domiciled (see 13.2) within the UK.

1.3   Income tax

Income tax is, not surprisingly, a tax on income. What is meant by 'income' and how is it calculated in order to establish what your tax liability might be?

The system for assessing your 'income' to income tax commences with calculating how much that income is. Tax law has special rules for establishing what is to be considered as income and how it is to be added up. The different sorts of income which are taken into account are as follows:

(a)   Income which you receive from rent in respect of land and buildings (but not necessarily from furnished lettings) — Schedule A.

(b)   The notional income which you receive from occupying

land when your purpose is to grow timber on it — Schedule B.

(c) Income from British government stocks and also certain similar investments overseas when the income is collected through a UK bank or similar institution — Schedule C.

(d) Income which you receive from all other sources except an employer — collectively grouped as Schedule D.

Schedule D is subdivided as follows:

Case I	Income from 'trades'.
Case II	Income which you earn from your profession or vocation.
Case III	Interest received.
Case IV and Case V	Income which arises to you from outside the United Kingdom (but not if you *earn* it while working in the United Kingdom or from an overseas employer). This would include rental income from a holiday home abroad.
Case VI	Income from anywhere else which is not covered by some other classification. (This includes, in particular, furnished lettings.)

(e) Income which you receive from an employer (and if you are a director of a company, even if you are the only shareholder, you are an employee of that company) — Schedule E.

(f) Dividends (and certain other payments) from companies within the UK — Schedule F.

1.4 Since fiscal year 1973/74 there has been a single system of income tax which applies to the total of all your income. Prior to that date there were two different administrations collecting tax, one of which collected the 'standard' rate of tax and certain lower rates — now all consolidated and called 'basic-rate tax'; and another independent administration which collected 'surtax' which applied to higher incomes. Many of the complexities of the present system date back to the separation of the tax assessment systems. What makes understanding the income tax system so difficult is that income tax is collected in different places and at different times. Although your income from all the various schedules and cases set out above must be added together to calculate how much tax you have to pay, it is still collected from you separately in respect of each different 'source'.

1.5 Indeed, unless you make a special point of it, you will find it very difficult to obtain from your Inspector of Taxes a statement on a single sheet of paper explaining how your income from the various sources has been added together and how your various allowances and tax rates have been allocated. If your income is at all complicated, you should ask your Inspector of Taxes for a Form 930 on which he will show you how he has calculated what tax you have to pay.

1.6 If you are employed, then your employer will act as a tax administrator on behalf of the Inland Revenue. He will deduct tax (and National Insurance contributions) from your earnings and, having deducted it, pay it over on your behalf to the Inland Revenue. You have no choice in the matter. You cannot choose to administer your income tax in relation to your employment yourself.

Many other sources of income which you may have are administered in such a way that basic-rate income tax is deducted or deemed to be deducted before you receive the income.

1.7 Income from outside the United Kingdom

Restrictions applied to the movement of money to and from the British Isles from 1939 to 1979. Since 1979, however, there has been no restriction on investment outside the UK, and one of the most popular investments has been a holiday home abroad. The rules for taxation of such a holiday home are explained in Chapter 13 but your holiday home, if you obtain rent from it, is only one of a number of sources of income which you might have from abroad. Your liability to UK taxation (unless you are not domiciled in the UK) in respect of such income is the same, whether or not you bring the money to Britain. In certain circumstances you may suffer local taxes on such income. If this happens your Inspector of Taxes will usually only collect UK tax from you to the extent that it exceeds the tax paid abroad. You should enjoy relief for overseas taxes suffered on the income either through the mechanism of a double taxation convention or through 'unilateral' relief.

1.8 How much income tax will you have to pay?

Income tax is levied on the following scale.

Band of chargeable income	Tax rate	Tax on the band	Cumulative tax
First £15,400	30%	£4,620	£4,620
Next £2,800 (up to £18,200)	40%	£1,120	£5,740
Next £4,900 (up to £23,100)	45%	£2,205	£7,945
Next £7,500 (up to £30,600)	50%	£3,750	£11,695
Next £7,500 (up to £38,100)	55%	£4,125	£15,820
Over £38,100	60%		

The scale is applied to your income as adjusted by deducting various allowances and deductions. The principal allowances are as follows:

	Available if you are:	1983/84 £	1984/85 £
Single personal allowance	Single, widowed, a widower, divorced or separated	1,785	2,005
Married personal allowance	In full if married for the whole of the tax year	2,795	3,155
Wife's earned income allowance	A married woman who receives earned income*	1,785	2,005
Additional relief for children	A single parent or a married man whose wife is totally incapacitated	1,010	1,150
Dependent relative relief**	Your or your wife's relative has low income: maximum will be		
	(a) Single women	145	145
	(b) Others	100	100
Widows' bereavement allowance	Widowed in the current fiscal year or in the prior fiscal year (and have not remarried)	1,010	1,150
Housekeeper relief	A widow or widower and have a relative staying with you as housekeeper or alternatively employ a housekeeper, not a relative (there are further restrictions)	100	100

Available if you are:	1983/84 £	1984/85 £
Blind person's allowance	Registered blind	360	360
	(If both husband and wife blind)	720	720
Son's or daughter's services	Aged or infirm and depend on your son or daughter who lives with you and whom you maintain	55	55

*Wife's earned income allowance. This is available only to the extent of the wife's earned income but the figures above are the maximum.

**Dependent relative. This term has a special definition used only for the purposes of this personal allowance and is not the same as the definition used elsewhere in this book.

1.8.1 If you or your spouse is aged over 65 then the single and married persons' allowances above are increased as follows:

	1983/84 £	1984/85 £
If single	2,360	2,490
If married	3,755	3,955
But to the extent that your income is more than	7,600	8,100
then these higher allowances are reduced by £2 for each £3 of excess until your income reaches:		
If single	8,462	8,827
If married	9,040	9,300

at which point you may claim only the ordinary single or married person's allowance.

Note that even if you are a woman aged over 60 (or your wife is) and drawing a state pension in her own right, until you (or, if married, one of you) is at least 65, you cannot claim the increased allowance.

1.9 Executors and trustees do not enjoy personal allowances in their capacity as executors or trustees, but this does not affect their own entitlements to such allowances.

If you are not resident in the UK you may not be entitled to all the personal allowances (for the rules see 12.13).

1.10 Apart from your personal allowances, you may also deduct from your income, before it is assessed to tax, certain amounts you spend. The more common of such allowable deductions are:

(a) Mortgage interest relief (see Chapter 2).
(b) Deeds of covenant to charities (not exceeding £5,000 p.a. gross).
(c) Payments to a separated or divorced spouse under a binding agreement or UK court order (if you are not domiciled in the UK you may be able to claim relief for alimony payments under a foreign court order in the same way as shown in 13.7).
(d) Losses from a trade or profession.
(e) Payments under deeds of covenant, entered into before 7 April 1965, to individuals.
(f) Premiums paid for personal pension plans.
(g) Losses arising from the management of woodlands on a commercial basis if you made a special election to that effect.

1.11 In calculating your income, you must include income arising from gifts by you which are enjoyed by your infant children, unless (a) they are resident in the United Kingdom but you are not, or (b) the income is less than £5.

1.12 Capital gains tax (CGT)

CGT applies to individuals, trustees or personal representatives if they are resident or ordinarily resident in the United Kingdom, during the fiscal year in which the gain arises. The rules for establishing the residence of *an individual* are explained in Chapter 12.

CGT is payable by individuals who are resident and ordinarily resident in the UK but domiciled elsewhere only in respect of gains arising within the UK or which, although arising elsewhere, are brought to the UK.

1.13 Trusts or settlements *(CGTA s. 52)*

In the case of *trusts or settlements*, they are treated as resident and ordinarily resident in the United Kingdom unless:

(a) a majority of the trustees are not so resident; and
(b) the general administration of the trusts is carried on abroad.

This rule does not necessarily apply to trustees whose business or profession includes the management of trusts, such as accountants, solicitors or trustee companies.

1.14 Personal representatives

Personal representatives are treated as if they were resident, ordinarily resident and domiciled wherever the deceased person whose estate they are administering was resident, ordinarily resident and domiciled.

1.15 What is chargeable to CGT?

The profit which you make when you sell property of any sort or

otherwise dispose of it (such as by gift or if it is lost by fire or
burglary and you receive insurance proceeds) is chargeable to
CGT at a flat rate of 30%. No charge arises on a disposal to your
spouse unless you are separated.

1.16   There are several exemptions of which the more
important are:

(a)   Your home in certain circumstances (see Chapter 8).
(b)   Private motor vehicles.
(c)   National Savings Certificates, etc.
(d)   Betting winnings including premium bonds.
(e)   Gilt-edged securities and certain corporate securities
      which you have held for at least a year or inherited (unless
      you repurchase them within a month of sale, when special
      rules apply).
(f)   Compensation for injury or damage to your profession or
      vocation.
(g)   The proceeds of sale, surrender or maturity of a life
      insurance policy, unless you purchased it from somebody
      else.
(h)   A gift to charity, or to the nation.
(i)   Any article valued at less than £3,000 (unless it was part of
      a set worth more than £3,000 given or sold to the same or a
      connected person at the same or any other time).
(j)   Any object (or animal) which is not fixed (such as a house)
      but which has a predictable life of less than 50 years. This
      might include a boat or aeroplane, a racehorse or a
      hogshead of wine.

1.17   Relief from CGT   *(CGTA, s. 5)*

An individual or a married couple is not chargeable to CGT for
the first £5,600 of gains made in any fiscal year, and this
exemption is given without taking into account losses made in a
previous year. If in 1983/84 you made losses for CGT purposes

of £10,000, but in 1984/85 you made gains of £4,000, you can claim exemption from CGT in 1984/85 and carry the losses from 1983/84 forward to use in later years if you then make gains. There is only one exemption of £5,600 for a married couple.

1.18 Losses and CGT   *(CGTA, ss. 5 and 45(2))*

When you dispose of an asset you might make a loss rather than a gain. If that happens you must deduct that loss from any gain you or your spouse makes in the same fiscal year (unless by 5 July following that fiscal year you have elected to be separately assessed to CGT, in which case your spouse's gains are not offset against your losses). Such an election does not, in practice, affect your liability to tax if you both make gains. If you and your spouse do not make gains equal to the total of your losses in that fiscal year you may carry the loss (or as much of it as is not used up by gains in that year) forward and set it against gains in later years. This will still apply if, in an intervening fiscal year, you have been abroad and so exempt from CGT. The losses in the years when you were resident can be used to reduce gains you might make after you return to the UK.

1.19 Losses on sales to connected persons

You cannot create a loss by selling an asset, which has fallen in value since you acquired it, to anyone who is connected to you; such a loss can only be deducted from a gain made on another disposal to the same person.

1.20 Who is connected to you for CGT purposes? *(CGTA, s. 63)*

(a) Your husband or wife, or the brother, sister, ancestor or lineal descendant of you or your husband or wife.

(b) The trustee of a settlement is connected with the settlor, or with anyone connected with the settlor.

(c) In respect of the disposal of partnership assets, a partner or spouse of a partner, unless the transaction was on an arm's-length basis.

(d) In the case of a company which you control (either alone or with others who are connected with you), you are connected to that company.

1.21 Transactions between connected persons *(CGTA, s. 62; ESC D6)*

If you sell or give an asset to a connected person, the price which you are treated as having received, is always market value. This applies even to a married couple who are separated until the time they are divorced; for that period the exemption from CGT on transfers between spouses does not apply (except in the fiscal year in which they separate), but they are still connected to one another. However, if *either* spouse continues to live in a property, then whichever spouse owns the property is treated as occupying it, so long as the owner does not have another *principal private residence*. Otherwise an unexpected charge to CGT can arise if a home is transferred as part of a divorce settlement. This can be deferred, however, by making *a holdover election*.

1.22 What is a hold-over election? Who can make it? And what does it do? *(FA 1980, s. 79; FA 1981, s. 79)*

If a charge to CGT might arise as a result of a disposal not for full value (a gift or a transfer to or from a settlement), then the charge can be 'held-over' if an election to do so is made before the end of the sixth fiscal year following the disposal. Broadly, the effect of the election is that the recipient of the asset (the transferee) is treated for CGT purposes as having acquired the asset subject to a deferred liability to CGT on the 'held-over' gain. This is the gain on which CGT would have been paid, at the time of the transaction, by whoever made the disposal (the transferor).

1.23 The result is that no charge to CGT arises to the transferor on the transfer, but the held-over gain gives rise to a charge to CGT on the transferee when he disposes of the asset (unless he in turn signs a hold-over election with the recipient). A charge would also arise if the transferee becomes neither resident nor ordinarily resident within six fiscal years after the end of the fiscal year in which the original disposal took place; but this charge is held in suspense for three years if the occasion for the charge is that he takes up full-time employment abroad. In those circumstances the charge is not made if, within the three years, he has returned to the UK and not disposed of the asset in the meanwhile. The charge is payable in the first place by the transferee, on the basis that he is deemed to have disposed of the asset on the day he ceases to be resident (see 12.8); if he does not pay the tax within 12 months of its being assessed it can be collected directly from the transferor.

1.24 The election to hold-over a gain must be made jointly by both parties. The transferee must, at the time of the transfer, be either resident or ordinarily resident in the UK. On a transfer *to* a settlement the election may be made by the settlor alone.

If, as a result of the transfer, a charge to CTT also arises, then any CTT paid on the transfer (whether paid by the transferor or the transferee) is allowed, to the extent it does not exceed the held-over gain, as an addition to the cost of the property for CGT purposes when it is ultimately sold or disposed of by the transferee.

2 *Interest paid*

If you borrow money to buy or improve or develop your home, then you may claim to deduct the interest you pay from your taxable income, so reducing your income tax liability. The way in which this relief is calculated varies depending amongst other things on how much you borrow and from whom, and whether you occupy a single home or own more than one.

2.1 What is a home? *(FA 1972, sch. 9)*

In order for you to claim relief for interest paid, the money must be borrowed *to acquire* (see 2.3(a)) land or an interest in land (such as, for example, a leasehold flat or house), or a caravan or houseboat, which is to be used as your home. The term 'land' includes anything which stands on the land, for example a house. The land must be in the United Kingdom or the Republic of Ireland (and not elsewhere such as the Channel Islands, France or Spain). Non-domiciled individuals (see 13.6) may be entitled to claim relief for interest paid on homes elsewhere (see 13.7).

In order to qualify for relief the home must be used *when the interest is paid* as the only or main residence (see below) of either:

(a)   the borrower; or
(b)   his or her divorced or separated spouse (see Chapter 6); or
(c)   a dependent relative (see 2.11).

or be used for that purpose within 12 months of the money being borrowed. You can ask the Board of Inland Revenue (through your Inspector of Taxes) to extend this period of 12 months in appropriate circumstances. This might apply if, for instance, you were having difficulties in selling your previous home or the building of your new home was taking longer than 12 months.

2.2 Warning note

Some people think that if you borrow money secured on a mortgage on your home then interest paid will qualify for relief. Unfortunately this is not always the case even if your home satisfies the tests laid out above and the sum you borrow is within the limits explained in 2.5. The right to tax relief is not given because you have used your home as security, *but only if the money you borrow is used for a specified purpose.*

2.3 What is a specified purpose? *(FA 1974, sch. 1)*

The law sets out the following as specified purposes:

(a) The acquisition, improvement or development of your home (to satisfy this test the money must be borrowed within a reasonable time of when you spend the money — three months before *or after* the time you spend will be accepted as reasonable).

(b) The acquisition, improvement or development of land let commercially (see 7.14).

(c) The purchase of a home annuity (see 2.19).

(d) The purchase of an interest in a trading or professional partnership for use in the business, or the purchase of plant or machinery for business if you are an active partner.

(e) The purchase of ordinary shares in a close company which is not simply an investment company, or a loan to such a company to use in its business if you own at least 5% of the ordinary shares in the company *or* work full time in the conduct or management of the business.

(f)   The purchase of plant or machinery if you hold an office or are employed and you use the plant or machinery in your work.

(g)   The loan to personal representatives of money so that capital transfer tax can be paid before 'grant of representation', but relief is only given for one year.

(h)   Money borrowed to replace other borrowings which were for any of the above purposes.

2.4   Example 2A

Your friend, Mr McLeod, suggests you join him in partnership to run a fish and chip shop. You have owned your home for many years and have no outstanding mortgage. You will have to invest £5,000 in the partnership. Your house is worth £30,000. You approach your bank manager and say you would like to borrow £5,000 to invest in the venture. He asks for a charge on your house and says you may borrow up to £10,000. You borrow £5,000 immediately and put it into the partnership with Mr McLeod. A few months later, it is your son's 21st birthday and you would like to buy him a car; you borrow a further £2,000 from the bank, using the existing facility.

The interest you pay on the £5,000 will be allowable for tax but not the interest on the £2,000 which you borrow to buy your son's car.

In practice, you would have only one loan of £7,000 so that you would claim relief on the interest you pay multiplied by 5,000/7,000.

You could apportion the interest for the period when you only borrow £5,000 as follows:

    1 April 1984   Borrow £5,000.
    1 July 1984   Borrow £2,000.
    30 July 1984   Bank charges £200 interest on the whole loan.

You have borrowed:

    £5,000 for 3 months
    £2,000 for 1 month

You may claim tax relief on:
$$£200 \times \frac{5,000 + 5,000 + 5,000 + 5,000}{5,000 + 5,000 + 5,000 + 7,000} = £181.82$$

2.5 How much relief may you claim? *(FA 1974, sch. 1, para. 5)*

2.5.1 If the amount which you borrow to buy your home is not more than £30,000, you will be entitled to claim all the interest which you pay to the lender as allowable for tax purposes. If you pay interest under the MIRAS scheme (see Chapter 3) you will already have been allowed tax relief at the basic rate of tax (30%), but if you also pay tax at higher rates, then you will be entitled to further relief for that interest.

2.5.2 The loans on which you may claim relief are restricted to £30,000, but if you enjoy an interest-free loan from, say, a relative then that may be ignored. It may, however, be taken into account in calculating any benefit you may enjoy if you also have an interest-free loan from your employer (see 10.12).

2.5.3 If you borrow more than £30,000, then your relief is restricted. The way in which the restriction is calculated is to add all the loans raised *at the same time* on which you pay interest (and which have been used to buy your home) to find what your

total borrowing is. Next you add the gross interest which you
pay on all those loans. (The gross interest you pay will be 10/7
multiplied by the net interest you pay either under the MIRAS
scheme or if you have to deduct tax because the lender is abroad
or alternatively the actual interest you pay if you do not deduct
tax.) The allowable interest will be restricted by the formula:

$$\text{gross interest} \times \frac{£30,000}{\text{total loans}} = \text{allowable interest}$$

2.5.4 Example 2B You bought your house in 1978 for
£40,000 and borrowed £25,000 from your building society,
£5,000 interest free from your Uncle George and £10,000 from
your bank.

In 1983 your building society told you that from 5 April 1983
they would apply the MIRAS scheme to your loan.

The interest which you pay in the 12 months ended 5 April 1985
is as follows:

Building society: MIRAS	£1,837.50
Uncle George	nil
Bank	£1,200.00

The amount on which you may claim relief is calculated as
follows:

	£
Total loans: ignore loan from Uncle George (interest free)	
£25,000 + £10,000	35,000
Gross interest:	
Building society (MIRAS) £1,837.50 × 10/7	2,625
Bank	1,200
	3,825

Allowable interest:

$$\frac{30,000}{35,000} \times £3,825 = £3,278.60$$

2.5.5 Some Inspectors of Taxes will *wrongly* calculate the allowable interest differently (and to your disadvantage). They will calculate that your non-allowable interest is interest *on* £35,000 less £30,000, so say you may only claim:

$$\text{building society interest} + \frac{£10,000 - £5,000}{£10,000} \times \text{bank interest}$$

which would give a total of only:

$$£2,625 + \frac{£1,200}{2} = £3,225 \text{ allowable interest}$$

This calculation is not correct if you borrowed from the building society and from the bank at the same time.

2.5.6 The Inspector would be quite correct if you had borrowed £10,000 from the bank not when you bought the house but say in 1984 to add an extension. The rule is that loans for home purchase or improvement which, added to your previous borrowings for those purposes, exceed £30,000 will be limited by a fraction calculated as follows:

Allowable interest on new loan must not exceed

$$\frac{(£30,000 - \text{previous loans})}{\text{new loan}} \times \text{interest on new loan}$$

You can see that if previous loans exceed £30,000, no relief will be given for interest on further loans.

2.6 Home for a dependent relative

The maximum borrowing to buy your own home and that of one

or more dependent relatives on which interest relief may be claimed is £30,000; if the total exceeds £30,000 the interest on the two loans you pay will be restricted. If you already have a loan on your own home of say £25,000, and borrow a further £20,000 to buy a home for a dependent relative (see 2.11) then the interest on the two loans will be restricted as if you had borrowed a further £20,000 to buy or improve your own home.

2.7   Example 2C

Assume interest on your original loan was 10% and interest on the new loan is 12%. The calculation would be:

Allowable interest on your own £25,000 mortgage   £2,500
Allowable interest on later £20,000 borrowed:

$$\frac{(£30,000 - £25,000)}{£20,000} \times £20,000 \times 12\% \qquad\qquad 300$$

Allowable interest   £2,800

2.8   Borrowing for other purposes

If before borrowing £20,000 to buy a home for, say, your widowed mother you borrow £10,000 secured on your own house, say, to subscribe for shares in the company of which you are a director, then the interest you pay on the earlier borrowing is allowable for tax *and the borrowing is ignored in calculating relief on the later borrowing* to buy a home for your widowed mother.

2.9   Bridging loans   *(FA 1974, sch. 1, para. 6)*

If you want to move home you may find that you have to pay interest on your new home before you have sold your old home and paid off your old mortgage. In these circumstances you may enjoy tax relief on the loan on both homes for a period of 12 months (or longer if you can show that the longer period is reasonable because, for example, you cannot sell your old home), but not if you sell your new home without moving into it first.

In the case of bridging loans *each* loan is eligible for relief up to £30,000.

2.10 Borrowing from a bank

If you raise a bridging loan from a bank make sure it is a loan and not an overdraft, because no tax relief will be given for overdraft interest. Make sure your bank manager marks the lending as a loan. The same rule will apply to money which you borrow, for example, to build an extension to your home. At the end of each tax year you should ask your bank for a certificate of the interest you have paid for tax purposes (a form MIRAS 5) which you should send to your Inspector of Taxes.

2.11 A dependent relative's home *(FA 1974, sch. 1, para. 1(4))*

If you borrow money to provide a home for a dependent relative, then you may claim that the interest you pay is allowable for income tax just as if you had borrowed the money to buy your own home. The amount of money you borrowed is treated as part of your maximum borrowing (see 2.6).

However, relief would not be given in the case of, say, a home for old people run by a charity which asks for an interest-free loan before it will accept an old person as a resident. If you borrowed money to help a dependent relative to find such a loan, you could not claim tax relief for interest you pay on your borrowing (because you do not acquire property rights in connection with the loan).

2.12 Definition of 'dependent relative'

The term 'dependent relative' has a special meaning in the case of interest relief. To qualify as a dependent relative the person concerned must *not* pay you rent and:

(a)   must be your or your spouse's relative; and
(b)   must live rent free and without any other consideration in his or her home; and
(c)   must be incapacitated by old age or infirmity from maintaining himself or herself; though if she is your or your spouse's mother, she need not be incapacitated if she is widowed, divorced or living apart from her husband.

2.13   Dependent relative's own income

There is no requirement that a 'dependent relative' is in any way financially dependent on you — the relief is not restricted however big his or her income might be.

2.14   Interest relief and capital gains tax

If you look at 8.22 you will see that there are similar rules for capital gains tax if homes are occupied by dependent relatives. (See also 11.13 for DLT relief.) There are, however, two important differences in the rules:

(a)   Relief may be given for interest paid on the home of more than one dependent relative.
(b)   Relief for interest paid stops on the death of the dependent relative.

2.15   What is a form MIRAS 5 and how can it help you reduce your income tax liability?   *(SI 1982 No. 1236)*

Since the introduction of MIRAS (Chapter 3), a new certificate of loan interest paid has been designed so that lenders such as building societies, banks and insurance companies can certify in a standard form what interest you have paid them, whether tax has been deducted from all or part of that interest, and how much of the loan was outstanding at the end of the year. The certificate also shows how much interest you are expected to pay in the following year.

You should ask whoever lent you money to help you buy or improve your home to provide you with a form MIRAS 5 at the end of each fiscal year. When you receive it you should complete the section headed 'Purpose for which loan is used' appropriately. (You will see from 2.2 and 2.3 that interest paid on a mortgage is not always qualifying interest, hence the question.)

2.16   The MIRAS 5, when you have completed it, should be sent to your Inspector of Taxes with your tax return as it will give you the formal entitlement to income tax relief which you claim. If you pay interest gross, not through MIRAS, your Inspector may not give you tax relief until he has received the MIRAS 5.

2.17   Job-related accommodation   *(FA 1974, sch. 1, para. 4A; FA 1977, s. 36)*

If your employer provides you with a home which you occupy as 'job-related accommodation', then there are two circumstances in which you may be able to claim relief for interest you pay on money borrowed to acquire *another* home:

(a)   If the other home has been purchased with the *intention* that it becomes in due course your *only or main residence.*

(b)   If, at some time during that fiscal year, it is used as *a* (but not necessarily the main) residence which you occupy. In the first 12 months after you borrow the money, you must occupy the property at some time even if not in the fiscal year in which you purchase it.

The rules for representative occupation (see 10.8) apply equally
to restrict your entitlement to interest relief for income tax, so
that, in particular, living accommodation provided to someone
by a company of which he is a director (or any associated
company) will not be 'job-related accommodation' unless:

(a) He (and his associates) control less than 5% of the
     company; *and*
(b)   (i)   he is a full-time (at least 25 hours a week but check
             with your Inspector of Taxes if in doubt) working
             director; or
      (ii)   the company neither carries on a trade nor do its
             functions consist wholly or mainly of holding
             investments or other property; or
     (iii)   the company is established for charitable purposes.

The restriction in respect of directors does not apply where the
job-related accommodation is provided for security reasons.

2.17.1 Do you live in job-related accommodation?   You
can determine whether your home is job-related accommodation by answering the questions in Figure 2.1.

2.18   What if you have two homes?

If you have two homes, then you may only claim as deductible
for tax the interest paid on money borrowed to acquire one
home and then only if, *as a question of fact*, that home is your
main residence. Unlike the rules for capital gains tax (see 8.6),
you cannot choose which home qualifies for relief.

This means that if your home has no mortgage and you want to
buy a holiday home, you will not be able to claim tax relief on
money you borrow to buy the holiday home — even though that
is your only mortgage. If, however, you subsequently move to
live most of the time in what was your holiday home, you can
then claim relief on interest you pay on the mortgage.

Figure 2.1

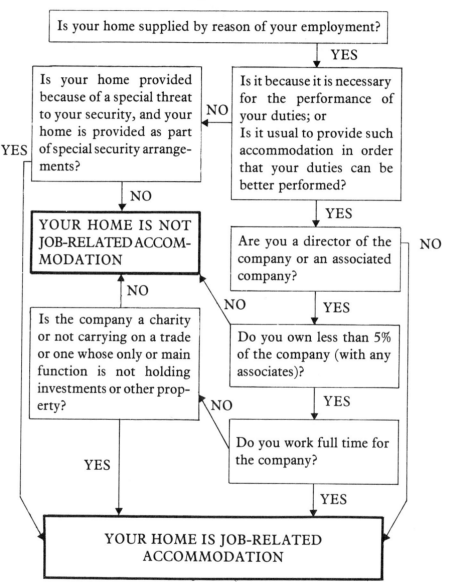

You cannot enjoy relief for interest you pay if your main residence is rented and you borrow money to buy another home which is not your main residence. The exception to this rule is if you live in job-related accommodation and you intend to move later to the home you are now buying, in order to occupy it then as your sole or main residence (see also 12.17).

2.19   What is a home annuity?   *(FA 1974, sch. 1, para. 24)*

For many retired people, their home is their only or main asset. At the same time, they find they do not have sufficient income to cover their living expenses.

A home annuity is an arrangement whereby such people can borrow money secured by a mortgage or charge on their home and, at the same time, be sure that they can continue to live there. Another arrangement is to sell the home but retain the right to live there rent-free as long as they live. In both cases, the money raised is used to provide the extra income.

Both arrangements make use of the special tax treatment of 'purchased life annuities'. If you pay a capital sum to an insurance company, they will pay you a fixed income for as long as you live. This scheme is known as a purchased life annuity. Because part of the 'income' is your own capital being repaid, that part is tax-free in your hands.

2.20   If you or your spouse is more than 65 years old and you borrow up to £30,000, *secured* on your sole or main residence, and you apply at least 90% of the money to purchase a 'purchased life annuity', then interest you pay on the money you borrow is tax deductible. If it is borrowed from a building society, the society will operate the MIRAS scheme (see Chapter 3).

These schemes really work best for the elderly. Probably they will not be worthwhile to you if you are less than 70 years old if single; if you are a married couple, you should both be at least 75. This is because it is only then that annuity rates are high enough to cover the interest payments and leave enough money over to produce a worthwhile income.

The two schemes differ. In one you continue to own your home so that if it increases in value, the increase belongs to you or your heirs. In the other, there is an outright sale of your house and any increase belongs to the financial organisation which makes the arrangement with you.

These schemes are a gamble on how long you will live. If you make the arrangement and die shortly afterwards, the insurance company will keep the money and make a quick profit. But if you live to a ripe old age, they will lose.

2.20.1 Example 2D You are a single woman aged 75 and your home is worth £30,000. Under one scheme you can borrow about 80% of the value of your house. Suppose you decide to borrow £19,500. This would increase your *net* spendable income by approximately £1,450 p.a. (if you do not have to pay higher-rate tax).

2.21 The building society or other lender expects to be repaid from the proceeds of the sale of your home after you die. If you have no one particularly to whom you want the value of your home to go after your death, this may not worry you at all. What matters to you is to enjoy more income now and still to live in your home.

The schemes usually incorporate provisions to deal with the situation in which you may want to sell your home and buy another or perhaps move into more sheltered accommodation.

2.22   Interest paid after your death   *(FA 1974, sch. 1, para. 8)*

If you die owning your own home with a mortgage still outstanding on it, your personal representatives will have to continue paying interest until the mortgage is repaid.

They may claim to deduct such interest from income which arises to them if, when you died, either of two conditions was satisfied:

(a)   the home was your sole or main residence; or
(b)   you lived in the property or intended that it should become your sole or main residence and meanwhile lived in job-related accommodation.

Such a claim may be made for so long as either your surviving spouse, or a person who was your dependent relative, satisfies either of these two conditions for himself or herself in respect of the property.

2.23   Joint borrowers   *(FA 1974, sch. 1, para. 23)*

If two or more people purchase a property together (other than married couples for whom special rules apply, see Chapter 6) then, for so long as the property is the sole or main residence of any one of them, he or she may claim tax relief on interest paid on a loan, whether sole or joint, up to a maximum of a £30,000 loan each. If a married couple buy a home jointly with someone else — perhaps the widowed mother of one of them — then the married couple jointly may claim relief in respect of £30,000 and the other individual can similarly claim.

Relief for interest paid on a joint loan is given to whoever actually pays the interest and is not restricted to a mathematical apportionment of the interest based on the share each has in the property, subject to the overriding £30,000 limit. The relief is apportioned according to the proportion of the interest paid by each borrower.

2.24 Cooperative Housing Associations *(FA 1981, s. 25)*

Relief is extended to members of approved cooperative housing associations if they lease their homes from the association and the *association* pays interest on money borrowed to purchase or build the property, provided the individual would be entitled to the relief if he or she personally owned the property concerned.

2.24.1 Example 2E You and your wife live with your widowed mother and decide to buy a new home which you adapt to provide a granny flat for your mother. The cost will be £55,000. You borrow £25,000, your mother borrows £10,000 and she puts up £20,000 from her own money to provide the balance. The house is bought jointly by all three of you. The interest rate payable in 1983/84 was, say, 11%.

If you pay 11% of £25,000, i.e., £2,650, you will enjoy full tax relief on it. Your mother in turn pays 11% of £10,000, i.e., £1,100, and she enjoys full tax relief on that.

In 1984/85, your mother finds she cannot keep up her share of the mortgage interest, so you pay it in full. The tax relief which you enjoy will be limited to:

$$\frac{£30,000}{£25,000 + £10,000} \times (£2,650 + £1,100) = £3,214.$$

3 Mortgage interest relief at source (MIRAS)

As has been explained in Chapter 2, income tax relief is given for interest paid on money borrowed to acquire or improve your home. The way in which this relief is given to you (in contrast to the amount of the relief which you enjoy) will depend on, amongst other things:

(a) From whom you borrow.
(b) How much you borrow.
(c) The purpose for which you borrow.
(d) Whether you are resident in the UK.

3.1 *(FA 1982, s. 26)*

The new rules concerning mortgage interest relief at source (known as MIRAS) were introduced with effect from the fiscal year commencing 6 April 1983.

3.2 The majority of lenders of mortgage finance, such as building societies, banks and insurance companies are authorised by the Inland Revenue to operate the MIRAS scheme. At the same time the option mortgage scheme was abolished and new rules were introduced so that the MIRAS scheme gave, broadly speaking, the same advantages to low or nil rate taxpayers as the previous option mortgage scheme.

3.3 If your lender is one of those institutions authorised by the Inland Revenue to operate the MIRAS scheme, then for each full fiscal year during which the lender expects you to pay interest to it, you will pay the interest element of your mortgage repayments net of basic-rate tax; you will be treated by your own Inspector of Taxes as if you had already paid basic-rate tax on the mortgage interest which you pay.

3.4 If, for example, the interest rate you expected to pay to your building society on a loan of £24,000 was 10%, you might have expected that the interest you pay the building society would be £2,400. In fact the building society only asks you to pay £1,680 interest and credits you with having paid the £720 (£2,400 × 30%) which is the basic-rate tax which you have already deducted. Arrangements have been made between the Inland Revenue and those institutions who operate MIRAS by which the institutions recover from the Inland Revenue the tax which you are treated as having deducted and paid over to the Inland Revenue.

3.5   What is the advantage of the MIRAS scheme?

The real reason that the tax law was changed to introduce the MIRAS scheme was to avoid the necessity for your Inspector of Taxes to change your code number every time the building society or other lender changed its interest rate to you. For most taxpayers who pay income tax only at basic-rate, the change to the MIRAS scheme means that no future adjustment to their code number will be necessary.

With the change to MIRAS most employed people no longer see any reference to their mortgage interest payment in their annual coding notice, which they received usually in January in respect of the fiscal year to follow. It is easy to see how much simpler administratively for the Inland Revenue this change is.

3.6   What if you pay tax at higher rates?

If you pay tax at more than basic rate, even if you do pay your mortgage interest under the MIRAS arrangements, you will find a reference to mortgage interest relief in your coding notice. It is, however, a little difficult to work out how the figure you see in your coding notice relates to the interest which you pay. How does the Inspector of Taxes work out, in these cases, what should appear in your coding notice?

3.6.1 Example 3A If, for example, your Inspector calculates that you will pay tax at a top rate of 45% and you pay net interest of £2,100 through MIRAS, he will calculate your coding allowances as follows:

	£
Allowable interest gross: £2,100 × 10/7	3,000
Tax relief to be enjoyed: £3,000 × 45%	1,350
Enjoyed already through MIRAS: £3,000 × 30%	900
	450

3.6.2 He would then calculate how much income you would need to earn at your top rate of tax to pay £450 tax, which would be £1,000. The figure added to your code number which you would see in your notice of coding (representing 10% of the figure to be relieved) would be 100.

3.6.3 In the above example, if half-way through the tax year the rate of interest which the building society charges changed, then the Inspector would have to recalculate your coding notice. He would only have to do that if you pay more than basic-rate tax.

3.7 The calculation of your code number may also be important if one or more lender does not operate the MIRAS scheme.

3.7.1 *Example 3B*   In example 2B the interest payable was:

Building society (MIRAS): £1,837.50 × 10/7   = £2,625
Bank (gross)   £1,200

The Inspector must first calculate how much interest you may claim, which is (see Example 2B) £3,278.60. Suppose you are a basic-rate taxpayer. You have already enjoyed relief for £2,625 through MIRAS, so you are entitled to £3,278.60 – £2,625 say £654 further interest relief, and the figure which will appear in your coding notice is 65 (£654 ÷ 10).

If, however, the highest rate at which you pay tax is 50%, your code number will be calculated as follows:

	£
Tax relief on total allowable interest:	
£3,278.60 × 50%	1,639.30
Already given through MIRAS:	
£2,625 – £1,837.50	787.50
To be given through coding notice	£851.80

He would then calculate how much income you would need to earn at your highest rate of tax to pay £851.80 tax, which would be £1,704 and the figure by which your code number would be increased in your notice of coding would be 170 (£1,704 ÷ 10).

3.8 Two or more lenders

Should you have loans from two or more lenders you are still entitled to income tax relief on those loans provided that the loans qualify for income tax relief and the total amount owed does not exceed the statutory limit, currently £30,000. If they do exceed £30,000 then you will only receive income tax relief on the first £30,000.

Where the total of your loans does not exceed £30,000, you are entitled to operate MIRAS on the payments made to both lenders. Should a subsequent loan from another lender take the total debt over £30,000, and provided that loan was for a purpose which qualifies for income tax relief, the Inland Revenue will normally allow the existing loans to remain in MIRAS. The new loan would not be eligible for MIRAS and you would have to claim for relief in respect of that part of the loan which takes your total debt up to £30,000. This relief would be given through your PAYE coding or tax assessment.

3.9   Two or more borrowers   *(FA 1982, sch. 7, para. 6)*

If a mortgage loan is made to joint borrowers (other than husband and wife) for an amount in excess of £30,000, then the loan will fall within the MIRAS scheme (provided the purpose of the loan was to purchase or improve what was the only or main residence of *both* of them) provided that the share of each of them in the loan did not exceed £30,000.

3.10   Who are the lenders who operate the MIRAS scheme?

There are a number of groups of institutions who operate the MIRAS scheme. These are as follows:

(a)   Building societies.
(b)   Banks.
(c)   Local authorities.
(d)   Authorised insurance companies.
(e)   Sundry other lenders who have specific authority from the Inland Revenue. If you are not sure if the lender from whom you wish to borrow is within the MIRAS scheme, ask.

3.11 What if your loan exceeds £30,000? *(FA 1982, sch. 7, para. 5)*

If you borrow money, from a lender who operates the MIRAS scheme, a sum in excess of £30,000 to acquire your home, then the lender may choose whether or not to apply the MIRAS scheme to that loan. There are two possibilities:

(a) that you will pay interest under the MIRAS arrangements up to £30,000 and any interest in excess of that will be paid gross; or

(b) that you pay interest gross and tax relief on interest you pay on the first £30,000 of your borrowings will be given through your coding notice or tax assessment.

3.12 How does it affect you whether or not your mortgage payments are made under the MIRAS scheme?

When the MIRAS scheme was first introduced and came into effect from 5 April 1983, many people who had mortgages were confused by the changes which they found were being made to the payments they made to their lenders and to the tax which they paid. The effect of the MIRAS scheme was merely to transfer the tax relief from your coding notice directly to you. In simple terms you paid more tax than you previously had done on what you received from your employer and exactly the same sum was deducted from the payments you made to your building society or other lender. The situation now is that if you are an employed person you are no better and no worse off under the MIRAS scheme now than you were under the arrangements which existed before April 1983. If your building society applied the 'constant net repayment' system (3.20) on the change, you may have suffered a net increase in your total monthly payments which would have been compensated in later years.

3.13 There is one group of people, however, who have had a
slight improvement to their financial affairs as a consequence of
MIRAS. Self-employed people (who pay their income tax in
two half-yearly instalments, on 1 January and 1 July), did not
receive any benefit from notices of coding under the
arrangements before MIRAS came into effect. As a consequence, when MIRAS was introduced they enjoyed a 'tax
holiday' in respect of the tax which they deducted under the
MIRAS arrangements for the year 1983/84. A similar effect will
be enjoyed now by an individual who ceases to be employed and
becomes self-employed. In practical terms there is usually a
period of time which could be as long as nine months (if you
commence your self-employed source of income on 6 April in a
fiscal year) before you first have to account for income tax on
your source of self-employed income, and during this time you
continue to be entitled to pay your mortgage interest payments
with the benefit of the tax relief under the MIRAS
arrangements.

3.14 MIRAS and low incomes   *(FA 1982, s. 26(5))*

Before 1983, some people who wished to buy their own home
found that they did not enjoy the benefit of tax relief on
mortgage interest payments because their taxable income was
not high enough to bring them within the tax net. Such
individuals could choose to pay a special lower rate of interest
and the government would make up the difference to the lender,
but under that arrangement the borrower was not given tax
relief for the interest which he paid. This arrangement was
called an option mortgage.

These option mortgage arrangements ended with the
introduction of MIRAS because the net payments required
from the borrower under the MIRAS scheme were, broadly
speaking, equivalent to the payments which these borrowers
would have made under the old option mortgage scheme.
Provided the borrower occupies the property as his or her sole or

main residence, under the MIRAS scheme the Inland Revenue does not seek to collect from the borrower the income tax which the borrower has notionally deducted from interest payments made.

3.15   When will the MIRAS arrangements come into effect if you take out a new mortgage?

When you arrange your mortgage, you will be sent a form MIRAS 1, which should be completed and sent back to the lender, the MIRAS arrangements will take effect from the completion of the loan unless a contrary instruction is received from your Inspector of Taxes by the lender. But there are some cases, particularly if you are self-employed, when the Inspector will instruct the lender to defer applying the MIRAS rules for some period. Such a delay is not under the control of the lender. If this happens, the lender will require you to pay your mortgage payments with interest payable gross until the necessary approval is received, and only then switch to MIRAS arrangements. In such a case be sure to claim tax relief for the interest you pay. The form MIRAS 5 (see 2.15) will show whether and to what extent you have paid your interest gross or net.

3.16   Under what circumstances might the lender not operate the MIRAS scheme?

There are circumstances including some where the loan is for a qualifying purpose (see 2.3), in which your lender will not operate the MIRAS arrangements and will then send you a form MIRAS 3 for completion.

(a)   If the purpose for which the money is borrowed is not to acquire your sole or main residence. Suppose, for example, you approached your building society or your bank to advance money to you so that you might buy a holiday home in the country. If the general economic climate were appropriate, it might be that they would lend you funds for such a purchase. Because the property which you buy will not be your sole or main home, such a loan would not fall within the MIRAS arrangements and you would have to pay interest to the lender gross. As explained in 2.18 you would not in any event be entitled to mortgage interest relief for such borrowing.

(b)   If the money which you borrowed was to buy a property which was both to be your home and your place of business or work. An example of this sort of a borrowing would be if you purchase a shop with a flat over. Your bank may be perfectly happy to lend you money to acquire it, and for the reasons explained in 2.3 and 16.7 you would probably enjoy tax relief on all the interest which you paid on money borrowed to acquire the property. Despite this such a loan would not fall within the MIRAS arrangements.

(c)   If the loan is more than £30,000, but see 3.11 above.

(d)   If the loan is to finance repairs and not improvements (see 14.12).

3.17   Under what circumstances might a loan be removed from the MIRAS arrangements?

There are several circumstances in which a loan which previously had been under the MIRAS arrangements would be taken out of those arrangements.

One example would be if the property which you purchased no longer was your sole or main residence. Perhaps you moved to another part of the country, kept what was your former home and purchased a new one. The lender of the money you borrowed to buy your first home would be likely to demand that you stop paying mortgage interest under the MIRAS arrangements.

Another circumstance in which a lender might insist that your arrangements were taken out of the MIRAS scheme would be if your borrowing from that lender exceeded £30,000 because, perhaps, you borrowed more money to improve your home. Some lenders might be prepared to apportion the interest as explained in 3.11 and other lenders might effectively create a second mortgage loan on their books to segregate the loan which continues to enjoy MIRAS arrangements (the original loan) and a second loan in connection with which it was necessary to pay mortgage interest gross.

Another circumstance in which building societies and other lenders under the MIRAS scheme will insist that the borrowing is taken out of MIRAS will be if you are required to move abroad so that you no longer live in what was previously your home so that you are 'not resident' in the United Kingdom (see 12.2).

3.18   What sort of mortgages fall within the MIRAS scheme?

There are no restrictions which apply to the type of mortgage which falls within the MIRAS scheme. The same arrangements would be made whether your mortgage is a repayment mortgage, an endowment mortgage, a pension mortgage or a mortgage raised in connection with a home annuity.

3.19   Does MIRAS affect the way in which tax relief is enjoyed over the term of a mortgage?

The agreed period of repayment for a mortgage, usually called the 'term' of the mortgage, is usually fixed at the time when you take out your mortgage. If you take out a 'repayment' mortgage from a building society, you may find that if interest rates rise the building society will be prepared to extend the term.

3.20   In the case of repayment mortgages there are two

alternative ways in which building societies may calculate your monthly payments. The most common arrangement is called the 'constant net repayment mortgage'. Under this the capital and interest elements of your payment are spread evenly over the term. With such arrangements the *net* monthly payment which you make will remain the same over the whole term of the loan (assuming interest and basic tax rates do not change).

3.21   Some building societies and other lenders will offer loans under another scheme known as 'rising net repayment or "gross profile" mortgage'. Under these arrangements, again assuming no change in interest rates, the net payments which you make to the building society are lower at the beginning of the mortgage and higher at the end. The reason for this is that over the term of your mortgage you are repaying capital, so that the amount of interest which you pay each year falls. In the case of the rising net repayment mortgage, the building society or bank calculates how much you would pay them each month if you did not fall under the MIRAS arrangements, and paid equal monthly instalments throughout the term. This monthly instalment is then recalculated each year to adjust for the tax you deduct under the MIRAS scheme, usually varying the amount of your monthly net payments each year. Under these arrangements, you are repaying the capital a little more slowly in the earlier years of the term. The result is that net payments are lower in the early years of the term, but higher in later years, than under the constant net repayment mortgage.

3.22   MIRAS and job-related accommodation

If you live in job-related accommodation (see 2.17), and purchase a home with the intention of living there in the future, you should enjoy the benefits of MIRAS in respect of the money you borrow to buy your home, even if it is rented out, whilst you live in the job-related accommodation.

4 Mortgages from building societies

If you borrow money from a building society to buy your home then there are a number of ways in which the repayment of your borrowing may be arranged.

4.1 You may pay regular instalments which consist both of interest and capital repayments. Over the period of the mortgage the repayments of capital will be sufficient to repay the whole amount borrowed (the 'repayment' method).

4.2 You may, however, pay interest only to the building society, making arrangements with some outside financial institution, acceptable to the building society, to accumulate a capital sum to repay the amount you borrow at some date in the future.

4.3 The two common ways in which you might accumulate such a capital sum and which are acceptable to many building societies are:

(a) By taking out an endowment policy with an insurance company (the 'endowment' method).
(b) From the anticipated capital sum which you can expect by commuting part of your pension when you retire ('pension mortgage').

4.4   Home annuities

If you have borrowed from the building society to finance a home annuity (see 2.19) then the building society will allow the sum borrowed to remain outstanding until your (and your spouse's) death: the sum borrowed will be repaid when your home is sold after your death, so that during your lifetime you pay only interest on the amount borrowed.

4.5   Repaying your mortgage

Whatever method you choose to repay your mortgage, there are two elements:

(a)   Interest payments.
(b)   Repayments of capital.

So far as concerns the interest element of what you pay, your entitlement to claim tax relief for the interest you pay is exactly the same whether you pay your repayments under MIRAS or gross, and whether the mortgage is more or less than £30,000. The rules are explained in Chapters 2 and 3.

4.6   Tax relief and a repayment mortgage

If your mortgage is a repayment mortgage, then because the amount of your mortgage outstanding (that is, not yet repaid) reduces each year, the interest which you pay will be a smaller amount each year (assuming that the rate of interest does not change).

The less the interest you pay, the smaller the amount on which you are entitled to tax relief.

4.7   If your repayment mortgage is through the MIRAS scheme, your building society may calculate your repayments in such a way that the net amount you pay them each month is fixed, although the proportion of each payment which is interest and which is capital changes.

4.8   If you are a basic-rate taxpayer throughout the term of the mortgage, you will not notice the change in the tax relief, but if you pay tax at higher rates then you will find that each year your code number is changed as explained in 3.6 to reflect the lower interest element of your repayments.

4.9   Tax relief and non-repayment mortgages

If your mortgage is an endowment mortgage, a pension mortgage or a home annuity then the interest you pay each month remains unchanged throughout the term of the mortgage (unless interest *rates* change), so your entitlement to claim tax relief on the interest you pay also remains unchanged.

4.10   The tax treatment of the way you *repay* your mortgage is very different for the various types of mortgage.

4.10.1   Repayment mortgages   You can claim no tax relief or benefit for that part of your monthly payments which is used to reduce your mortgage.

4.10.2   Endowment mortgages   You will not obtain any tax relief for premiums which you pay towards an endowment policy which you take out after 13 March 1984 in order to accumulate capital to repay your mortgage. If you took out an endowment policy before that date, then the Inland Revenue would have given you tax relief of 15% by paying to the insurance company an amount equal to 15/85ths of the premiums which you pay to the insurance company, provided your policy was what was known as a 'qualifying policy'. Almost all endowment policies taken out in connection with mortgages before 14 March 1984 were 'qualifying policies' and so there was an element of tax benefit from repaying your mortgage through the endowment arrangement. This tax benefit will continue for policies taken out before 14 March 1984. If you have such an insurance policy, even if it is not used now in connection with your mortgage, do not cancel it — you may want to use it at some time in the future in connection with a mortgage.

4.10.3 There are two parts to an endowment mortgage: the loan itself which is usually from a building society, a bank or an insurance company, and the endowment policy which you take out to repay that loan.

4.10.4 In the case of an endowment mortgage you would pay interest payments on the loan of a fixed amount each month to the lender and premiums to an insurance company on an endowment policy. The policy is designed in such a way that at the end of the mortgage term it will provide enough money to repay the money which you have borrowed at the beginning of the term, usually with a little bit extra.

Endowment policies taken out after 13 March 1984 do not enjoy the tax reliefs explained above, but for higher-rate taxpayers there may still be tax advantages in the accumulation of funds within an insurance policy.

4.10.5 *Example 4A* Comparison of repayment and endowment mortgages. Interest rate assumed 10.25% for repayment, 10.75% for endowment. Man aged 39. Sum borrowed £20,000. 25-year term. Norwich Union Minimum Cost Mortgage plan assuming 80% of current annual compound bonus. Policy taken out after 13 March 1984.

30% **Taxpayer**

	Repayment mortgage £		Endowment mortgage £
Net monthly payment to lender (MIRAS)	145.28		125.42
Mortgage protection policy (non-smoker)	8.20	Policy premium	29.80
Net monthly cost	153.48		155.22
At end of 25 years: Surplus cash on policy	nil		3,196.00
Further bonus which would be paid on similar policy maturing today	nil		9,230.00

60% **Tax payer**

	Repayment mortgage		Endowment mortgage
Average monthly repayment	178.97	Monthly gross payments of interest	179.17
Mortgage protection policy	8.20	Policy premium	29.80
Less: *Average* tax relief	67.38	Tax relief	107.50
Average net monthly cost	119.79	Net monthly cost	101.47
At end of 25 years: Surplus cash on policy	nil		3,196.00
Further bonus which would be paid on similar policy maturing today	nil		9,230.00

4.10.6 Pension mortgages The term 'pension mortgages'
is applied to circumstances where the building society or other
lender accepts that you may repay your mortgage not from the
maturity proceeds of an endowment policy, but from the tax-
free sum which you anticipate from a self-employed pension
arrangement (or personal pension plan). It is not a special
scheme for people who want to buy a house during retirement!

4.10.7 Some building societies and banks are prepared to
allow your loan to be linked with an approved personal pension
plan issued by an insurance company. These policies are
available to you only if you are self-employed or if your
employer does not provide a pension scheme for you (other than
the state pension arrangements which are ignored).

If you are self-employed, or if you think it is unlikely that your
employer will provide you with a pension scheme during the
period of your employment, you are entitled to contribute up to
$17\frac{1}{2}\%$ (or more, if you were born before 1917) of your earnings
each year to a 'personal pension plan'. The premiums which you
pay are deductible for tax.

Furthermore, the insurance company to which you pay the
premiums is wholly exempt from tax on money which it earns
on the money which is accumulated to provide your retirement
benefits. Such schemes are very attractive, and they may be
used to repay your mortgage in the following way.

4.10.8 *(ICTA, s. 226; FA 1971, s. 20)* Under the special
rules which apply to personal pension plans, you may draw your
benefits at any time between the ages of 60 and 75. When you do
draw your benefits, you may take *a proportion* tax free by way of
a commutation of your pension. The rule is that you may draw
tax-free an amount not exceeding three times the pension which
remains.

It is the prospective tax-free lump sum which your building
society, bank, insurance company or other lender will look to, at

the beginning of the mortgage term, to repay the mortgage at the end of the term (which must of course be when you are at least 60). If your career is one which commonly ends at less than 60, for example if you are a professional footballer or an opera singer, the Inland Revenue may allow a younger age than 60 for you to draw your pension (and so have the opportunity to take a tax-free lump sum).

4.10.9 The lender will usually be conservative about estimating how much you may enjoy as a tax-free lump sum; a common formula is 80% of the insurance company's own projection, excluding any terminal or vesting bonus.

4.10.10 From a tax point of view, pension mortgages are very attractive because you enjoy tax relief not only on the interest which you pay, but also on the accumulation of capital to repay the mortgage. There are, however, some pitfalls:

(a) You may not be eligible throughout the term of the mortgage to pay premiums on a personal pension plan. If you cease to be self-employed or change jobs and your new employer has a compulsory pension scheme (as, for example, most public service employments) or your present employer introduces a compulsory pension scheme, you may not be entitled to maintain your personal pension plan. It might be necessary then to switch to a repayment mortgage which might then require high monthly repayments because it would be for a shorter term.

(b) You have to use some of your pension benefits to repay the mortgage when you retire, so you will enjoy less money during retirement.

(c) The monthly outgoings will be higher than for a repayment mortgage.

4.10.11 If however you are self-employed and likely to remain so until you are 60 (in such professions as barrister, vet, chiropodist, solicitor, doctor, practising accountant or dentist) then it is worth considering the advantages of a pension-linked mortgage, particularly if you are not paying as much as you are entitled to under Inland Revenue rules towards a self-employed pension.

4.10.12 Example 4B Comparison of repayment and pension mortgages. Interest rates assumed 10.25% repayment, 10.75% pension mortgage. Man aged 39. Sum borrowed £20,000. 25-year term. Norwich Union Pension Mortgage Plan assuming current bonus rates are maintained.

30% Taxpayer

	Repayment basis £			Pension mortgage £
Net monthly payment to lender (MIRAS)	145.28	Interest (MIRAS)		125.42
Mortgage protection policy (non-smoker)	8.20	Term Assurance (non-smoker)		7.80
		Pension premium		42.35
				175.57
		Less: Tax relief		
		Term assurance	2.34	
		Pension premium	12.71	15.05
Net monthly cost	153.48			160.52
At maturity	nil		See below	

60% **Taxpayer**

Average monthly			
repayment (gross)	178.97	Interest paid	179.17
Average tax relief	67.38	Tax relief on	
		interest @ 60%	107.50
	111.59		71.67
Mortgage protec-		Term Assur-	
tion policy	8.20	ance	7.80
		Pension	
		premium	42.35
			50.15
		Tax relief	
		@ 60%	30.09
			20.06

Average net		Net monthly	
monthly cost	119.79	cost	91.73

At maturity	nil	See below

The pension policy at maturity would provide sufficient funds to give the following benefits:

(a) A tax-free lump sum of £24,999.
(b) From the tax-free lump sum you would repay £20,000 mortgage, leaving you £4,999 tax-free cash in your hands.

plus

(c) A pension of £7,405 p.a., guaranteed to be paid for as long as you live and in any case five years.

A similar policy maturing today would provide benefits of a tax-free sum of a further £9,504 and further pension of £2,816.

5 *Borrowing other than from building societies*

There are many lenders, other than a United Kingdom building society, from whom you might borrow money and the way in which you will obtain tax relief in respect of the interest which you pay will vary depending upon who the lender is.

5.1 Borrowing from a United Kingdom bank

If you raise your money to purchase your home from a United Kingdom bank, and the amount that you borrow does not exceed £30,000, then the MIRAS scheme will operate, which is explained in Chapter 3.

However, the MIRAS scheme will not operate if the total amount you borrow is greater than £30,000, or if you borrow from a bank which does not itself operate the MIRAS scheme. You will then be required to pay the interest gross.

5.2 You will not, however, enjoy any tax relief for interest paid to a United Kingdom bank if you borrow money in the form of an overdraft (unless the money has been borrowed to acquire or improve a home with a view to carrying on your business from it — see 16.7 — in such a case the interest you pay will be treated as an ordinary business expense).

It is therefore very important to ensure that the bank understands the purpose for which you are borrowing the money and agrees that the money will be advanced to you as a loan rather than as an overdraft. The problem can arise if your bank is providing a bridging loan (see 2.9). You should make sure that what you are given is in fact a loan and not an overdraft.

If you do borrow money from a bank on a loan account to assist you with the acquisition of your home, whether the loan is a bridging loan or a loan which is outstanding for a longer period of time, in order to obtain tax relief you must ask your bank to provide you with a form MIRAS 5 at the end of each fiscal year. This is a certificate of loan interest paid and without this certificate your Inspector of Taxes will not give you tax relief for the interest which you have paid.

When you have obtained the form from the bank you must complete it and state the purpose for which you have borrowed the money and then attach it to your tax return before sending it to the Inspector of Taxes.

5.3   There is one important difference between interest paid to building societies and interest paid to banks. In the case of building societies you do not have to put on your tax return the amount of interest which you have paid to the building society but merely your 'roll number'. The building society will have advised your Inspector of Taxes of the amount of interest payable in respect of your mortgage, and relief would have been given to you for that amount. In the case of a bank you have to enter the amount paid.

5.4   Borrowing from an insurance company

There are circumstances in which you may borrow money from an insurance company (or a company connected with an insurance company) for the purpose of acquiring or improving your home.

5.4.1 Borrowing against the value of an insurance policy Most United Kingdom insurance companies, which sell endowment or whole life policies, include in the policy terms arrangements by which you may borrow from the insurance company, against the security of the value of the policy, once premiums have been paid for a specified period of time. In most cases the insurance company will lend approximately 95% of the surrender value of the policy at that time. The surrender value in the early years of the policy is likely to be considerably less than the premiums which you have already paid in connection with it. These provisions often do not apply to 'unit-linked' endowment policies.

5.4.2 If the insurance company will lend you money against the value of your policy then that borrowing may well be used by you as part of the total money you borrow to acquire your home or improve it. In some cases the policy will have written into its conditions a specific right for you to borrow money against the surrender value at a rate of interest which is (a) fixed and (b) less than you would have to pay to another lender such as a bank or building society. If the total money which you borrow from all lenders to acquire your home exceeds £30,000, and part of the total borrowing either to acquire (or subsequently to improve) your home is to come from a low-cost source of borrowing such as some insurance companies, it is worthwhile making sure that the money which you borrow from the insurance company is the last tranche of money which you borrow. As explained in 2.5.6 there may be a restriction in respect of the allowability of interest for the last slice of your borrowing, and it is worthwhile making sure that any interest for which you do not obtain tax relief is the least expensive interest which you pay.

When you pay interest to an insurance company and you claim tax relief in respect of the interest, ask for a form MIRAS 5 because your Inspector of Taxes will require evidence of the interest which you have paid. He will not normally be satisfied merely that you have paid a similar amount of interest in the previous year and will require evidence each year of the payment of interest.

5.4.3 Insurance companies and 'top-up' mortgages If you have borrowed to acquire your home from two lenders simultaneously, very often you will have borrowed a basic sum from a building society and an additional amount known as a 'top-up' from another lender who is very often either an insurance company or a finance company associated with the insurance company. The building society will probably operate the MIRAS scheme unless your borrowing from them exceeds £30,000, but the 'top-up' borrowing may not be subject to the MIRAS arrangements.

You should obtain from the 'top-up' lender, whether it is an insurance company or an associated finance company, a form MIRAS 5 which you should send to your Inspector of Taxes each year.

5.4.4 In the case of a 'top-up' arrangement with an insurance company, you will almost certainly have been required to take out an endowment policy either on your own life or on the joint lives of your spouse and yourself. The tax treatment of such life insurance premiums is explained in 4.10.2.

5.5 Borrowing from a private lender

You may borrow all or part of the money you require to acquire, or extend or improve your home from a private individual, perhaps a relative, rather than from a financial institution, such as a bank, insurance company or finance company. As explained in 2.5.2, if you do *not* have to pay interest on such a loan, then for the purpose of calculating the maximum loan in respect of which tax relief may be claimed, the loan is ignored. It could well happen that the loan is interest free if you have borrowed the money from a relative or friend who is well disposed towards you.

If the borrowing from the private individual concerned bears interest, however, it is treated like any other borrowing so far as your entitlement to tax relief on interest paid is concerned, unless the interest paid is to a lender who is not resident in the United Kingdom for tax purposes (see 12.1), in which case special rules apply, see 5.6.

5.5.1 *Example 5A*

Suppose your wealthy Uncle George says he will help you buy your home. The home you wish to buy costs £30,000 and he says he will lend you £10,000 to help you buy it. He says he will charge you only 5% interest on the money which you borrow from him. In each year you will pay Uncle George £500 interest and you should not deduct any tax before paying it to him. You will have to satisfy the Inspector of Taxes that you have paid the interest so it will be a good idea to obtain a receipt from Uncle George each year. He, of course, will have to pay tax on the receipt of interest from you and you may well find that your Inspector of Taxes will delay granting you relief on the interest paid to Uncle George until he has satisfied himself, by cross-checking with Uncle George's Inspector of Taxes, that Uncle George is indeed paying tax on the interest he receives from you.

You would be entitled to the same tax relief if the house for which you are claiming tax relief is not the one in which you yourself live but a house occupied by a dependent relative. If Uncle George was unable to work because of his age, and you had no home which was your sole or main residence, it could even be that the house for which you claim interest relief, which you financed with money borrowed from Uncle George, is occupied by Uncle George as your *dependent relative*.

5.6 Borrowing from a non-resident lender *(ICTA, s. 54)*

If you pay interest to a lender who is not a resident of the United Kingdom for tax purposes (see 12.1) then regardless of the purpose for which the money is borrowed you must deduct tax before paying the interest to the lender if the interest which you pay is 'annual interest'.

5.6.1 There are two important exceptions to this rule:

(a) If the lender is a foreign bank which has a branch in the United Kingdom and you borrow from the United Kingdom branch.

(b) If the lender is a resident of a country which has a double-taxation treaty with the United Kingdom under which interest may be paid without deduction of tax (the lender then is subject to tax on the interest in the country of residence). The countries which have such a treaty with the United Kingdom are:

Austria
Denmark
Faroe Islands
Finland
Federal Republic of Germany
Greece
Hungary
Republic of Ireland
Luxembourg
Malawi
Netherlands
Netherlands Antilles
Norway
Poland
Sweden
Switzerland
United States of America

5.6.2 Under some treaties for the avoidance of double taxation, the rate of tax which is deducted before interest is paid is lower than the UK basic rate. These countries are as follows:

	Rate of tax to be withheld when making interest payments
Australia	10%
Bangladesh	10% ($7\frac{1}{2}\%$ to banks; nil to government bodies)

Barbados	15%	
Belgium	15%	
Botswana	15%	(nil to government bodies)
Canada	15%	
Cyprus	10%	
Egypt	15%	(nil to government bodies)
Fiji	10%	
France	10%	
Gambia	15%	(nil to government bodies)
Ghana	15%	
India	15%	(10% for some bank loans; nil to government bodies)
Indonesia	15%	(10% for some bank loans; nil to government bodies)
Israel	15%	
Jamaica	12·5%	(nil to government bodies)
Japan	10%	
Kenya	15%	(nil to government bodies)
Republic of Korea	15%	(10% on loans exceeding two years; nil to government bodies)
Malaysia	15%	
Morocco	10%	(nil to government bodies)
Philippines	15%	(nil to government bodies)
Portugal	10%	
Romania	10%	
Singapore	15%	
Sri Lanka	10%	(nil to banks)
Sudan	15%	
Thailand	25%	(10% for some bank loans; nil to government bodies)
Trinidad and Tobago	10%	(nil to government bodies)
Yugoslavia	10%	
Zambia	10%	

5.6.3 If you are paying interest to a lender in any of the territories in 5.6.1 or 5.6.2 you must deduct tax at basic rate until you have obtained confirmation from the Inspector of Foreign Dividends, Lynwood Road, Thames Ditton, Surrey, that you may pay the interest without deduction of tax.

Once you have his agreement to pay the interest without deduction of tax, you may continue to do so each year without having to apply separately for each payment.

5.6.4 How do you claim tax relief for payments made to a non-resident lender?

If you make payments of interest to a non-resident lender then you must deduct tax at basic rate and account for it separately to your own Inspector of Taxes before paying the interest. If you fail to deduct tax, then strictly speaking the Inspector of Taxes dealing with your affairs will require you to pay an amount of tax equivalent to three-sevenths of the net amount which you do in fact pay as interest.

If you borrow money from a lender abroad, make sure that the terms of the arrangements with the lender deal with the fact that you may have to deduct tax. Otherwise you may find that the interest cost of the borrowing is much greater than you thought it would be.

5.6.5 (SI 1970 No. 488)

When you pay interest to a lender abroad, you may claim as allowable interest the total of the amount you pay to the lender and the tax which you have to deduct on paying the interest to him as if the total of the two were the gross interest which you pay. There are special arrangements under which if you pay interest either gross or with a lower rate of withholding tax to a lender in a country having a double-taxation arrangement then you may claim tax relief on the gross interest which you pay even though you have not deducted tax at all or not at basic rate.

5.7 Replacing a loan *(FA 1972, sch.9, para.1; FA 1974, sch.1, para.5)*

Whoever you may have borrowed money from for the purpose

of acquiring or improving your home, it may be that circumstances arise subsequently that you wish to repay that lender and borrow an equivalent amount from some other lender to replace the sum which you borrowed. This might also be true for interest-free money which you borrowed (perhaps because the money was borrowed from your employer (see 10.12) or from a friend or relative who now needs the money back for some reason).

In such cases, whether or not you paid interest on the loan which you are repaying, interest paid on the loan taken out to repay the original loan will potentially be allowable interest provided that the total amount borrowed does not exceed £30,000.

The replacement loan is treated as having been made at the time the original loan which it replaces was made. If your total borrowings exceed £30,000, the replacement of a previously interest-free loan will alter the loans for which interest relief is granted.

5.7.1 *Example 5B* On 1 January 1980 you bought a house for £50,000, which you financed as follows:

	£
Building society	20,000
Interest-free loan from mother	10,000
Own funds	20,000
	50,000

On 1 July 1982 you extended your home at a cost of £10,000, which you borrowed from your bank on loan.

In 1983/84 the interest you pay is:

	Interest paid £
Building society £20,000 @ 10¼%	2,050
Bank £10,000 @ 11½%	1,150
Total borrowing £30,000	
Interest allowable	3,200

On 5 April 1984 your mother asks you to repay the loan, so you borrow a further £10,000 from your building society, with which you repay her.

In 1984/85 the interest you pay is:

	£
Building society £30,000 @ 10¼%	3,075
Bank £10,000 @ 11½%	1,150

As the further building society loan replaces the earlier loan from your mother, it displaces the loan from your bank; your total borrowings now exceed £30,000 and the earlier loans are relieved before later loans. Your allowable interest is limited to what is treated as the earliest £30,000 you borrowed, i.e., the loan from the building society so limiting allowable interest to £3,075.

5.8   Interest paid to vendors *(IR 11, para.20)*

It may be that when you buy your home you may have to pay interest to the vendor under the terms of the contract, either (a) because there are specific arrangements for delayed payment or (b) because you complete the purchase after some specified date or the vendor allows you to go into occupation before completion date.

If there are provisions for delayed payment such that a

proportion of the purchase price is left outstanding, then the vendor is treated as if he had made a loan to you. Interest payable under such an arrangement is treated as if the vendor had lent you the money to enable you to acquire the property.

If the interest becomes payable either because:

(a)   you complete after the contractual date specified; or
(b)   the vendor allows you to go into occupation before completion date,

then the interest paid is treated as if it were interest on a loan equivalent to the price outstanding under the contract; the provisions in respect of 'bridging loans' (see 2.9) will apply.

The same provisions will apply if you buy a plot of land from a builder who is to build a house on it for you and the builder allows you to delay paying part of the cost of the building for as long as you pay interest on the outstanding amount.

6 Marriage, divorce, separation and interest relief

The rules explained in Chapter 2 for claiming tax relief on interest paid are both expanded and adapted in the case of married couples. They also provide for the situation which may arise if a married couple divorce or separate.

6.1 Who is treated as a married couple?

If you are a married man and live with your wife, then as a couple you are usually treated (for the purpose of claiming tax relief on interest you pay) as a single unit, so that jointly you can have only one main residence and can only claim relief for interest paid on a total borrowing of £30,000 (see 2.5.1) for the acquisition of that home. There are some exceptions to this general rule:

(a) Special rules apply in the fiscal year in which you marry.
(b) There are special rules if one of the couple is non-resident but the other is resident in the UK (see 12.6).
(c) Extra restrictions may apply if you have elected for separate assessment of wife's earnings (see 6.4).
(d) The rules are extended if you have separated or divorced.

6.2 The year in which you marry *(ESC A38)*

It may be that when you marry, you already have a home for which you are claiming mortgage interest relief. What happens if both of you have such a home and mortgage? You might both sell your homes and jointly buy a new one. Together you might therefore have two or even three homes whilst you sell your previous home(s).

The Inland Revenue allow you to claim that a loan on a home which you are trying to sell should be treated as a bridging loan.

If you are trying to sell two homes and have two loans, then each loan is treated as a bridging loan (and a separate £30,000 limit applies to each loan) but only if the new home is being bought jointly.

In order to enjoy this extra relief:

(a)   The 'bridging loan' rules apply (see 2.9). The property being sold must be sold within 12 months of its ceasing to be the main residence of whoever lived in it and claimed interest relief on his or her mortgage. The period of 12 months may be extended if you can show the Board of Inland Revenue that there is good reason why they should grant an extension (perhaps a sale falls through or the property you are trying to sell is in a depressed area where no one wants to buy at the time).

(b)   If you both are selling your previous homes, the 12-month period starts from when you borrow the money to buy your new joint home.

6.3   Who pays the interest? *(FA 1974, sch.1, para.5)*

Generally, for a married couple who live together, it makes no difference who pays the interest on money borrowed to acquire a home even if the home was bought before the marriage. Within the limit of £30,000 borrowings, relief will be given in the way which pays you best.

6.3.1   Example 6A   In the year to 5 April 1985 you earn £10,000 p.a. as a local government officer. Your wife earns £2,060 p.a. as a playgroup assistant.

When you married you moved into a house which your wife had previously bought with the help of a £15,000 building society loan, and she has continued to pay the mortgage interest. The gross interest paid on the mortgage is £1,500.

The fact that your wife (and not you) pays the mortgage interest is not specially taken into account in calculating your joint tax liability, which is calculated as follows:

	£	£
Husband's income		10,000
Wife's earned income	2,060	
Less: Wife's additional earnings allowance	. 2,005	
		55
		10,055
Less:		
Married man's allowance	3,155	
Mortgage interest relief	1,500	
		(4,655)
Taxable		5,400
Tax payable at 30%		1,620

Note that although your wife pays the mortgage interest, she can still claim her full wife's additional earnings allowance.

6.4 Separate taxation of wife's earnings *(FA 1971, sch.4, para.4)*

If two people, each of whom has high earnings, are married, they may wish to be taxed, so far as concerns the wife's earned income, as if they were not married. The rules relating to mortgage interest relief when there is separate taxation of wife's earnings are very strictly observed and provide:

(a)   That the borrower may claim interest relief but only if he or she actually pays the interest.
(b)   That if the mortgage is joint then relief is given to whoever actually pays the interest.
(c)   That the wife's unearned income must be added to *her husband's* total income without any relief for interest which *she* pays on a mortgage.

6.4.1   Example 6B   In the year ended 5 April 1985, you earn £20,000 p.a. and your wife earns £6,000 p.a. Your wife has an income from investments of £3,000 p.a. You have a joint £30,000 mortgage, the interest on which is £3,000 p.a. gross.

Possibility (1): you do not elect for separate assessment of wife's earnings. Your tax assessment will be calculated as follows:

	£	£
Your earned income		20,000
Your wife's earned income		6,000
Your wife's unearned income		3,000
		29,000
Less:		
Your married man's allowance	3,155	
Your wife's additional allowance	2,005	
Mortgage interest relief	3,000	
		8,160
Joint taxable income		20,840
Tax payable		6,928

Possibility (2): *you* pay the mortgage interest and you and your wife jointly elect for separate assessment of her earnings.

Your assessments will be calculated as follows:

Your assessment	£	£	£
Your earned income		20,000	
Your wife's unearned income		3,000	
		23,000	
Less:			
Only a single person's allowance	2,005		
Mortgage interest relief	3,000		
		5,005	
Your taxable income		17,995	
Your tax payable			5,658
Your wife's assessment			
Her earned income		6,000	
Less: Her single person's allowance		2,005	
		3,995	
Her tax payable			1,198
Your joint income tax liability			6,856
Tax saved by election			72

What if the house and therefore the mortgage were only in your wife's name? If you elect for separate assessment of wife's earnings, she must pay the interest for her to be able to claim relief, and using the same figures as in the example above:

	£	£	£
Your earned income		20,000	
Your wife's unearned income		3,000	
		23,000	
Less: Single person's allowance		2,005	
Your taxable income		20,995	
Your tax payable			6,998
Your wife's earned income		6,000	

Brought forward	£	£	£
		6,000	6,998
Less:			
Single person's allowance	2,005		
Mortgage interest relief	3,000		
		5,005	
Her taxable income		995	
Her tax payable			299
Your joint tax bill has now increased to			7,297
Extra tax paid because of election			369

The same result would arise if your wife paid the interest on a joint mortgage. Do be careful before making an election for separate assessment of wife's earnings that you know who pays the mortgage interest!

6.5 If you separate or divorce *(ICTA, s.42; FA 1974, sch.1, para.1)*

If a married couple cease to live together because:

(a) they are separated under an order of a court of competent jurisdiction or by a deed of separation; or
(b) they are in fact separated in such circumstances that the separation is likely to be permanent (which is usually interpreted as living apart for a year); or
(c) they divorce,

then the rules explained in Chapter 2 governing the deductibility of interest are extended so that tax relief is given (still within the maximum borrowing limit of £30,000):

(a) On interest paid by one party to the marriage who does not live in the home, if the home is the only or main residence of the other party to the marriage; or

(b) On interest in fact paid by one party to the marriage who does live in the home which is owned by the other party. Tax relief is given in this case to an individual who neither owns the home nor is the borrower.

Note that if you neither own a property *nor* live in it you cannot claim tax relief in respect of mortgage interest *you* pay.

6.6 Divorce settlements: your home and tax

The general rule for regular maintenance payments is that they are allowable for tax purposes for the payer, and are taxable in the hands of the recipient. The payer must deduct tax at basic rate (30%) and pay this tax to the Inland Revenue. (The recipient may be able to claim back from the Inland Revenue all (or part) of the tax which has been deducted, if her total income is low enough.)

6.7 Suppose you and your wife separate. Your wife stays in the former matrimonial home. There are several ways in which the mortgage payments for the home may be made and they will have different tax consequences.

	Payments on which tax relief may be claimed	
	By husband	By wife
Husband keeps house, wife lives in it, husband pays mortgage interest	Mortgage interest	Nil
Husband transfers house to wife, husband pays mortgage interest not under court order	Nil	Nil

Husband keeps house, wife lives in it, wife agrees to pay mortgage interest	Nil	Mortgage interest
Husband transfers house to wife and agrees under court order to increase gross maintenance payment by amount equivalent to gross mortgage interest. Wife pays mortgage interest	Increase in maintenance payment	Mortgage interest

6.8   Relief for two mortgages

If the husband pays the mortgage interest himself, retaining an interest in the home, then that mortgage is part of his £30,000 maximum total mortgages (2.5). If, however, the wife assumes the whole burden of the mortgage and the husband agrees to increase his maintenance payments to cover the interest element of her mortgage then he will (indirectly) enjoy tax relief on the mortgage interest although the mortgage is his wife's and not his. This means that her mortgage is *not* part of his £30,000 maximum total mortgage. If he now buys a new home with a new mortgage, he may effectively enjoy tax relief on more than £30,000; if both mortgages were £30,000 he would enjoy tax relief:

(a)   On his own mortgage; plus
(b)   On the extra maintenance payment he makes to his separated or former wife to enable her to pay her mortgage interest.

6.8.1   *Example 6C* You have divorced your wife and had no children. You earn £35,000 p.a. gross. Your ex-wife earns

£2,000 p.a. gross. You agree to pay basic maintenance of £560 a month net, and to pay a further £140 a month net which is the exact total payment under MIRAS your ex-wife pays under her mortgage.

In 1984/85 you pay mortgage *interest* on your own home of £2,000 gross, and you establish that the gross *interest* element of your ex-wife's mortgage is £1,200.

Your tax is calculated as follows:

	£	£	£
Gross income		35,000	
Less:			
Maintenance payments			
12 × (£560 + £140)	8,400		
Tax deducted on payments	3,600		
	12,000		
Your mortgage interest	2,000		
Your personal allowance	2,005		
		16,005	
Taxable income		18,995	
	£		
Tax	15,400 @ 30%		4,620
	2,800 @ 40%		1,120
	795 @ 45%		358
	18,995		

Tax deducted from maintenance payments	3,600
Total tax payable	9,698

Your cash availability for yourself is:

	£	£
Gross earnings		35,000
Less:		
Net maintenance	8,400	
Tax payable	9,698	
		18,098
Husband's net spendable cash		16,902

Your wife's taxable income:

	£	£	Tax deducted at source £
Her earnings	2,000		Nil
Gross maintenance receivable	12,000		3,600
Gross taxable income	14,000		
Less:			
Her mortgage interest			

	£		
Gross	1,200		
Personal allowance	2,005		
	3,205		
Taxable	10,795		
Tax payable @ 30%		3,238.50	
Tax already paid under deduction		3,600.00	
Tax recoverable		361.50	

Her cash availability:

Net maintenance:	£
12 × (£560 + £140)	8,400.00
Own earnings	2,000.00
Tax recoverable	361.50
Cash availability	10,761.50

Each of you must, of course, pay his or her own mortgage repayments.

You obtain tax relief at your highest rate of tax, i.e., 45% on your gross payments to your wife, on which she pays only 30%.

6.9   Transferring your home to your spouse
(FA 1972, sch.9, para.8)

In order to prevent abuse of the rules for interest relief, you cannot claim relief for interest paid on a loan if you purchase your home from your husband or wife, unless you are separated, nor can trustees of a settlement claim relief for interest they pay on a mortgage if they buy the home from you or your spouse. (For capital gains tax aspects see 1.21.)

7 Letting your home

For a number of possible reasons you may wish (or have) to let the whole or part of your home. Perhaps you want to let a room to a student, or you have to move elsewhere because of your job but want to keep your home. You might let your home furnished or unfurnished. If you let your home, or part of it, you need to advise your Inspector of Taxes; you will be subject to income tax on any profit you make. There are different rules to establish what profit you make in the various cases, and special rules about what happens if your expenses are more than your receipts. See also Chapter 8 for capital gains tax aspects.

Before considering the different cases in detail, it is worth considering the nature of the expenses, or outgoings, which you may set off against rents received.

7.1 General outgoings *(ICTA, s. 72)*

Whether your home is let furnished or unfurnished, you may claim as a deductible expense money you spend in connection with:

(a) Repairs or redecoration of the property, if the money is *paid* while the property is let.
(b) Premiums paid for insurance against damage caused by fire, tempest, flood, explosion, aircraft, subsidence, heave, etc., or against liabilities you might incur as a property owner (such as the risk of a tile falling off your roof and injuring a passer-by).
(c) Specific costs you agree to bear — perhaps you pay a

gardener to maintain your landscaped garden and it is a condition of the tenancy that you will maintain the garden — but you must not be paid a special extra amount to defray this cost.

(d) Agents' letting and collection fees, whether at the beginning of the tenancy or on renewal, and the costs of advertising your home to let.

(e) If you pay them, general and water rates.

(f) Legal fees incurred in letting the property or in collecting arrears of rent or seeking to remove unsatisfactory tenants.

(g) Money you pay to others who assist you in managing the property — whether a professional estate agent or a friend or relative. If you pay an accountant who prepares accounts in respect of the letting and perhaps agrees them with your Inspector of Taxes, his fees will be allowable as part of management costs.

(h) Lighting and heating costs not paid by the tenant. (If you provide a coin-in-the-slot gas or electricity meter for the tenant's use, you must include the cash taken as part of your receipts, but claim what you actually pay to the gas or electricity board.)

(i) If your home is a flat in a block of flats, your service charges and rent payable under *your* lease (do check that you are allowed to sublet under the terms of *your* lease).

(j) Cleaning costs.

(k) If you have to pay ground rent or a compulsory contribution to the maintenance of a conservation area or private road.

(l) Costs incurred in appearing before a rent tribunal or rent officer.

Certain expenses are *not* allowable, for example:

(a) Your costs of travelling to or from your let home (if, for example, you have moved elsewhere).

(b) Money you spend to *improve* your home whilst it is let (or even if not let).

(c)   Provision for depreciation or wear and tear of the fabric of your home, that is, roof, floors, walls, windows, sanitary equipment, boiler and central heating equipment. You may only claim for what you actually spend.

(d)   Any expenditure that you have recovered or will recover from an insurance company, or from anybody else, unless you bring the sum receivable into your receipts subject to tax.

(e)   Money spent before your home is first let (but see 7.2.1). It may be worth waiting until the property is tenanted before repainting the outside of your home or repairing that faulty chimney.

(f)   Money you pay to a tenant as compensation for vacating your home.

(g)   Interest. There are special rules which give *separate* relief for interest which is not allowable to an individual as an ordinary expense of owning or managing property (see 7.14).

7.2 For what periods can you claim general outgoings?

7.2.1 *Lease at full rent* (ICTA, s.72) If you let your home under a 'lease at full rent', which means that the rent payable by your tenant covers all your outgoings and the property was empty before you bought it (perhaps you expect to move there after a few years), then you may deduct money you spend in repairing the property *before* it is let and during periods between tenancies at 'full rent', and making good damage or wear and tear after the last tenant has left.

If you occupied the property before it was let, or the tenant was already there when you bought it, money spent before you bought it or moved out cannot be claimed as an expense.

If you receive a less than full rent, then you may not claim money spent other than during the time a tenant is in occupation.

If part of your home is let at full rent, then an equivalent proportion of outgoings will be allowed as an expense.

If the rent your tenant pays you is a controlled rent, then it will be treated as full rent if it was a full rent when it was fixed.

7.2.2 Tenant's repairing lease If the *tenant* is bound to keep the whole or the greater part of the premises repaired then that is a 'tenant's repairing lease'.

7.3 Sharing accommodation

If you let a room or rooms in your own home and you live there at the same time, then you may deduct a proportion of your general outgoings (see 7.1) from the rent your lodger pays to you. Exactly which specific outgoings you may deduct will depend on the terms under which the lodger stays with you. If, for example, you give him a cooked breakfast as part of the arrangement, then the cost of the food you provide may be deducted, but you may not, for example, deduct 'wages' for yourself for serving it to him. This is because you are not allowed to claim a deduction for the cost of your own time; however, if you have to pay somebody else to do this work, then you can claim what you have to pay them for the *extra* work they have to do because you have a lodger.

If you are a married man you could perhaps pay your wife for her work in cooking for, and cleaning, the room occupied by the lodger. The 'wage' you pay her would be an allowable expense for tax purposes and, if she had no other earned income, would be free from tax and national insurance contributions in her hands, provided in 1984/85 it was less than £1,690 p.a. (a figure higher than that is unlikely to be accepted as reasonable for such duties, in any case). Such a 'wage' must be for work she must do because you have a lodger, not for her ordinary household duties and not part of regular housekeeping that you would give her anyway. If you want to pay your wife and claim a deduction for what you pay her, it is a good idea to make a note of what she does and how much time it takes her (a rate of perhaps £1.50 to £2 per hour might be reasonable) since your Inspector of Taxes will probably enquire into the exact circumstances. You should also note the cost of any extra cleaning materials, for which you may also claim. It is important that you do pay the amount which you claim to your wife — it is not satisfactory just to claim the expense as a bookkeeping exercise.

7.4   General outgoings and shared accommodation

If you share accommodation, then you may deduct a reasonable proportion of your general outgoings. There is no hard and fast rule for calculating exactly what the proportion should be, but the most usual ways are:

$$\frac{\text{number of rooms occupied by your lodger(s)}}{\text{number of habitable rooms in your home}} \times \text{outgoings}$$

or

$$\frac{\text{area of your home occupied by your lodger(s)}}{\text{area of all habitable rooms in your home}} \times \text{outgoings}$$

If the lodger is only in the house for part of the year, you must reduce the proportion further by the factor:

$$\frac{\text{number of weeks lodger pays for}}{52}$$

7.4.1   Example 7A   You live in a house with three bedrooms and two reception rooms. You let one bedroom to a student for £16.00 a week, and the student pays rent for 30 weeks in the year. You provide breakfast as part of the arrangement, and calculate that the food the student eats costs you £3 per week. Your wife calculates she has to spend an extra four hours a week in cleaning and cooking, and you agree to pay her £1.50 per hour for this.

Your general outgoings on the house are £936 per year.

	£	£
Rent received: £16 × 30		480
Outgoings		
General outgoings:		

$$\frac{\text{Rooms let}}{\text{Rooms habitable}} \times \frac{\text{Weeks let}}{52} \times £936$$

	£	£
$= \dfrac{1}{5} \times \dfrac{30}{52} \times £936$	108	
Food: 30 × £3	90	
Wife's wages: 30 × 4 × £1.50	180	
	378	
Taxable income	102	

If you live in your home and let part of it, special capital gains tax concessions may apply (see 8.34) when you sell your home.

7.5 Furnished lettings

Most homes when let are let furnished, and some extra expenses are allowed in that case. Also the way in which the tax chargeable on your income from furnished lettings is assessed and collected is not the same as for unfurnished lettings. Furnished lettings are normally assessed under the provisions of Schedule D Case VI whereas unfurnished lettings are assessed under the provisions of Schedule A (see 7.6 and 7.8).

7.6   Furnished lettings: Schedule A or Schedule D?

If you include furniture, carpets, curtains, bed linen, crockery, etc., as part of the facilities for your tenant, then the rent you receive is partly in payment for the use of these items. It is more convenient both for the Inspector of Taxes and for you if the rent is taxed as a whole, but you may ask within two years of the end of a year of assessment for the rent to be divided between the payment for premises themselves (assessed under Schedule A) and the payment for use of the contents (assessed under Schedule D Case VI). You will see in paragraphs below that losses are treated differently under the two cases so that it may sometimes be advantageous to make a claim, but in practice this claim is rarely made.

7.7   Allowable costs in respect of furnished lettings
(SP A19)

In the past there were a number of ways in which your expenses incurred in connection with the provision of the contents of a furnished home might have been allowed for tax purposes. If in the tax year 1974/75 you had agreed a special basis you may continue to use it, but otherwise there are two possible ways in which you may claim relief. In no case may you claim the cost of equipping your home before it is let.

The bases you may now claim are:

(a)   Actual costs incurred in renewing or repairing any item which is broken or worn out (called the 'renewals basis').

(b)   A notional allowance of 10% of gross rent to cover the wear and tear of the contents. If the rent included items usually paid by tenants such as rates, these must be deducted from gross rents before the 10% is calculated.

Whichever of the two bases is used, it must be used consistently — you cannot, for example, claim 10% of gross rents in lieu of wear and tear and then also claim the costs of renewing a washing-machine.

7.7.1 *Example 7B*   In the year to 5 April 1984 you let your
home in Bristol whilst you are working in Newcastle for £90 per
week. Your cousin who lives in Bristol collects the rent each
week. (Generally, you may pay a collecting agent up to 10% of
the gross rent for weekly collections and this expenditure will be
acceptable to the Inland Revenue.) Your other expenses are as
follows:

	£
Rates	480
Water rates	100
Replacement curtains	300
Insurance	
House	120
Contents	80
Decoration	250
Gardener	200
Accountancy charges	80

The accounts could be prepared on the following alternative
bases:

Renewals basis	£	£
Rent received		4,680
Rent collection	468	
Rates	480	
Water rates	100	
Insurance		
House	120	
Contents	80	
Decoration	250	
Gardener	200	
Accountancy	80	
Replacement curtains	300	
		2,078
Furnished lettings: Schedule D VI income		2,602

Notional wear and tear allowance

Rent received		4,680
Rent collection	468	
Rates	480	
Water rates	100	
Insurance		
House	120	
Contents	80	
Decoration	250	
Gardener	200	
Accountancy	80	
Notional allowance		
10% × [£4,680 − (£480 + £100)]	410	
		2,188
Furnished lettings — Schedule D VI income		£2,492

Two points are worth noting. First that the notional wear and tear allowance usually will give a larger allowance than the renewals basis, and secondly that even if mortgage interest is paid it does not enter into the computation of Schedule D Case VI income — if paid it is given as a separate relief (see 7.14).

7.8   Schedule A and unfurnished lettings

If your home is let unfurnished, the income you receive will be assessed under the provisions of Schedule A.

You will be assessed provisionally in each fiscal year based on the amount of income (less expenses) actually received from letting your home in the *previous* year; the figure will be adjusted after the end of each fiscal year when the actual figures for that year are known. The tax, when provisionally assessed, is payable on 1 January *in* the fiscal year so that you must pay your tax before you have actually received all the rent on which you are assessed.

7.8.1 Example 7C In the year ended 5 April 1984 your assessable Schedule A income from letting your home was £2,000. In the year ended 5 April 1985 the assessable income is £2,300.

In about November 1984 the Inspector will raise an assessment as follows:

1984/85 Schedule A   £2,000

If you pay tax at 30% he will then show:

Tax payable @ 30%   £600 payable
             1 January 1985

When the figures for 1984/85 are finally calculated, the Inspector will raise a fresh Schedule A assessment, as follows:

	£
1984/85 Schedule A	2,300
Less: Previously assessed	2,000
	300
Tax payable @ 30%	90

In November 1985, or thereabouts, the Inspector will raise an assessment:

1985/86 Schedule A   £2,300 etc.

This £600 is payable on 1 January 1985, even though in February 1985 your tenant might leave the premises so that your income might be *less* than in the previous year.

If you have reason to think that your receipts will be less — perhaps because the property was empty for part of the year — you should tell the Inspector as soon as possible and he will then reduce the assessment as follows:

Amount assessable under Schedule A for preceding year ×

$$\frac{\text{estimated receipts (ignoring expenses) for current year}}{\text{receipts (ignoring expenses) for preceding year}}$$

If you have exceptional expenditure in a year so that your assessable income will fall, tell your Inspector of Taxes — strictly speaking he should not reduce his assessment but, in practice, he will accept an appeal against the assessment and a request for postponement of the tax payable on 1 January.

7.9   Losses: Schedule A

If your outgoings from letting your home exceed the rents you receive, then you may carry the deficit forward and set it against future income from the same source. If your home is let at full rent (see 7.2.1) but not if let on a tenant's repairing lease (7.2.2) then you may set the deficit on your home against any other Schedule A income you have from properties let on the same basis. If the property is let on a tenant's repairing lease, then the loss may be set against income from other properties let at a full rent but not under tenants' repairing leases.

7.10   Schedule D Case VI and furnished lettings
(ICTA, s.109)

Income from furnished lettings is included with other income from miscellaneous sources in the 'sweeping-up' category of Schedule D Case VI, which is the division of income tax legislation covering sources of income which are taxable but not covered elsewhere in the legislation. Some of the other sources of income which might be included under this category are:

(a)   Isolated literary activities — if, say, you sold a story to a newspaper.

(b)   Profits from transactions in Krugerrands — although you might think these were chargeable to capital gains tax, the

Inland Revenue sometimes argue otherwise.

(c)   Gains of a capital nature derived from disposals of land (other than your own home) where you acquired the land with the sole or main object of realising a gain of a capital nature (ICTA, s. 488).

All income chargeable under the provisions of Schedule D Case VI is added together in each tax year and treated as a single source, so if you have income from furnished lettings it will be included in such an assessment.

7.11   The income from furnished lettings (like income from all Schedule D Case VI sources) is taxable for each fiscal year on the actual income which you receive in that year, and the tax is payable on 1 January in that year. Because the Inspector of Taxes does not know before 1 January what your income for the year to the next 5 April will be, he will estimate how much your income is going to be, basing his estimate on what he already knows about what income you had in the previous year. In practice, he will probably estimate and assess that income as being a bit more than you had in the previous year.

7.11.1   Example 7D   In Example 7B above, your assessable income for 1983/84 was £2,492. In about November 1984 your Inspector of Taxes will probably raise an assessment as follows:

1984/85 Schedule D
Furnished lettings   E £2,750

The letter 'E' will tell you that he has estimated the figure which he expects you to receive for the year ending 5 April 1985. There is no obligation for him to tell you that he is estimating the figure but usually he will do so. He is obliged to estimate to the best of his ability what income you will enjoy from your furnished lettings. If you think he has overestimated, you should appeal against the assessment, giving the grounds for your appeal and asking for postponement of collection of that part of the tax which you think results from his overestimate of your income.

7.11.2   *Example 7E*   In example 7D above, your tenant who
had a tenancy at full rent, leaves the house in October 1984 and
you do not relet the property until December. After the
outgoing tenant has left, you find that he has left the house in a
bad state and you redecorate the hall and stairway at a cost of
£750; you estimate in December that you will receive £800 less
rent for the year because of the void period. You calculate that
your net income will be only £1,500. When in, say, November
1984 the Inspector raises an estimated Schedule D assessment
for 1984/85 in the sum of £2,750, you should, within 30 days of
the assessment being raised (the date of issue will be on the face
of the assessment and is not the day you receive it, which may be
several days later) appeal against the assessment.

The Inland Revenue provide standard forms on which appeals
may be made. Otherwise, your appeal should be worded along
the following lines:

> I appeal against your assessment reference No. —— in
> respect of Schedule D 1984/85 raised on —— November
> 1984 on the ground that because of lower rent received and
> higher repairs costs I estimate my income from furnished
> lettings for 1984/85 will be only £1,500. I also request
> postponement of £375 of the tax demanded.

In this example, the amount of tax postponed is calculated as
follows:

	£
Assessed by Inspector	2,750
Calculated by you	1,500
	1,250
Tax @ 30% × £1,250	375

7.12 Losses: Schedule D Case VI

If your income from letting your home is less than your outgoings, the shortfall becomes a loss for the purposes of Schedule D Case VI. You may deduct such a loss from any other Schedule D Case VI profit in the same year, or carry the loss forward against future Schedule D Case VI profits, whether from furnished lettings *or other sources* in future years.

You may not otherwise set off losses on letting your home, whether they are assessed under Schedule A or Schedule D Case VI, against income of a previous year nor can you claim to set such losses against income from any other source (such as your earnings or bank deposit interest) whether in the year you make the loss or in any other year.

Some people who have enjoyed income from furnished lettings in past years have claimed that their income from such a source was income from a trade and so classified as earned income, perhaps because of the amount of their own labour they personally have contributed, and these claims have been accepted. It has now been established in the High Court, however, that such claims were not acceptable in law, so even if you have enjoyed this treatment in past years, you will not enjoy it in future. You may find that your Inspector of Taxes will seek to review the tax treatment you have been given in past years. If this happens it is worth seeing an accountant or solicitor to find out whether the Inspector is entitled to do this. The rules are complicated.

New rules have been introduced this year, effective from 5 April 1982, which restore this more favourable tax treatment to the 'commercial letting' of 'furnished holiday accommodation' — see 7.16.

7.13 Interest relief *(FA 1974, sch. 1, para. 4)*

Mention has already been made earlier in this chapter that interest paid is not treated as an allowable expense in calculating your taxable income from your home. Instead a special set of rules applies to interest paid in connection with your home if it is let.

7.14 If you do not occupy your home as your only or main residence, then the rules which govern your right to tax relief, for interest paid on money borrowed to acquire your main residence, will not be applicable. If, however, your home is *let* you may claim relief for interest paid on money borrowed to acquire it in accordance with the rules set out in Figure 7.1. These rules apply only if the property is in the UK or Eire.

7.15 If the interest you pay is allowable in accordance with these rules, then there is no restriction on the sum borrowed; the sum you borrow is ignored in calculating the maximum amount which you may borrow in connection with the acquisition of your only or main residence.

In calculating whether interest paid in connection with *let property* will be allowable, you may apply the rules to any period of 52 weeks which need not be a fiscal year. For example, if you have a second home which you have not previously let, you may decide to let the property. From the date you put the property into the hands of agents as available for letting, you may claim interest paid in the following 52 weeks as allowable (even though it may take up to six months to let it), so long as it is actually let for at least 26 weeks in that period.

7.16 Furnished holiday accommodation *(FA 1984, s. 50, sch. 11)*

With effect from 5 April 1982, a new system of taxation has been introduced for 'furnished holiday accommodation'. If your

Figure 7.1 Tax allowability of interest paid

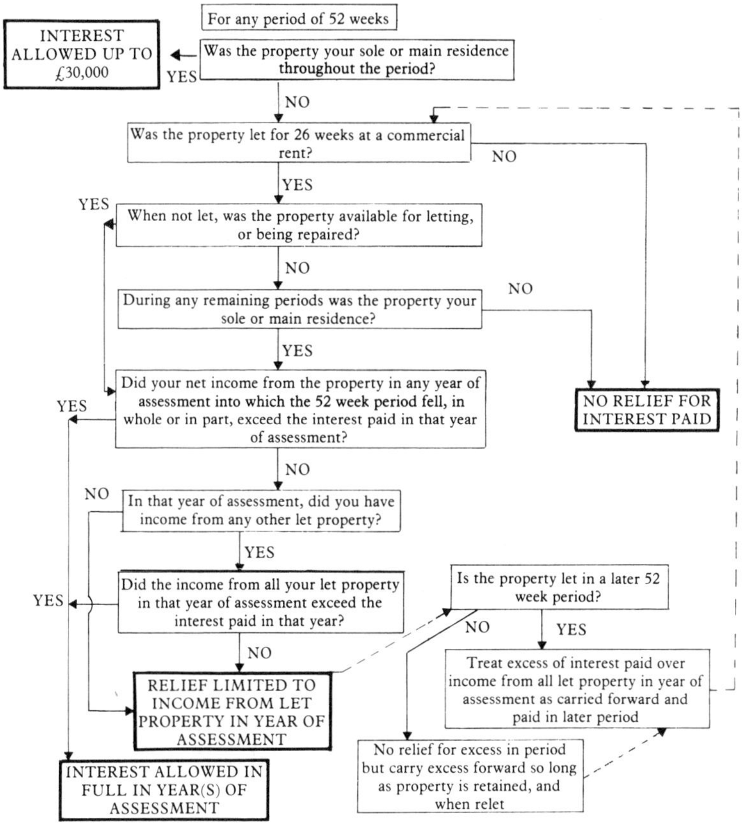

For any period of 52 weeks

INTEREST ALLOWED UP TO £30,000 ◄— Was the property your sole or main residence throughout the period? YES

NO

Was the property let for 26 weeks at a commercial rent? NO

YES

YES — When not let, was the property available for letting, or being repaired?

NO

During any remaining periods was the property your sole or main residence? NO

YES

YES — Did your net income from the property in any year of assessment into which the 52 week period fell, in whole or in part, exceed the interest paid in that year of assessment?

NO RELIEF FOR INTEREST PAID

NO

NO — In that year of assessment, did you have income from any other let property?

YES

YES — Did the income from all your let property in that year of assessment exceed the interest paid in that year?

Is the property let in a later 52 week period?

NO   YES

NO

RELIEF LIMITED TO INCOME FROM LET PROPERTY IN YEAR OF ASSESSMENT

Treat excess of interest paid over income from all let property in year of assessment as carried forward and paid in later period

INTEREST ALLOWED IN FULL IN YEAR(S) OF ASSESSMENT

No relief for excess in period but carry excess forward so long as property is retained, and when relet home falls within the new regulations, then income you receive from the 'commercial letting' of it is taxable under the provisions of Schedule D Case VI (see 7.10) but is treated as if it were trading income.

7.16.1 *What is the commercial letting of furnished holiday accommodation?* In order to come within the new regulations concerning commercial letting of furnished holiday accommodation, your home must satisfy all the following conditions:

(a) Be let on a commercial basis with a view to realising a profit from the letting; and

(b) Be let furnished so that tenants may use the furniture; and

(c) Be *available* for commercial letting to the public generally for periods which add up to at least 140 days; and

(d) Actually be let for at least 70 days; and

(e) For at least 7 months in total (which must include the periods it is actually let commercially) not normally be occupied by the same occupiers for a continuous period of more than 31 days.

The *period* in which these conditions must be satisfied is as follows:

To find out if, in any year of assessment, your letting qualifies, you must see if, in the preceding year of assessment, it was let by you as furnished lettings (whether as holiday accommodation or not). If it was, then the period to which the conditions apply is that fiscal year; if it was not let furnished, the period is the 12 months from when you let the property furnished in the year of assessment.

If, in the fiscal year *following* the year of assessment with which you are concerned, the property ceases to be let furnished, then the period to which the conditions apply is the 12 months ending when your furnished letting of the property ends.

If you own two or more properties in the same fiscal year, let as furnished holiday accommodation, you may average the periods which qualify.

7.16.2 If you satisfy all the conditions in paragraph 7.16.1 then:

(a) The income is earned income on which the tax is payable in two equal instalments (on 1 January in the year of assessment, and on the following 1 July);
(b) Losses on other furnished accommodation may be set against the income from the furnished holiday accommodation;
(c) You may pay premiums towards retirement annuity contracts based on such income (see 4.10.7);
(d) You may claim capital allowances in respect of any plant or machinery used in connection with the letting;
(e) You may claim rollover relief for capital gains tax in respect of gains made on the sale of the property or money invested in such a property (see 16.12);
(f) You may claim retirement relief on a disposal of the property (see 16.18).

7.16.3 *Losses and furnished holiday accommodation* In addition, if you make a loss in respect of the running of furnished holiday accommodation, you may claim to set off such losses against any other income you may enjoy in the same fiscal year. Alternatively, for the first three years in which you let property as furnished holiday accommodation, losses you incur may be set against your income of a fiscal year three years earlier; this alternative may not be applied if the property was first let as furnished accommodation by you (whether as furnished holiday accommodation or not) at any time more than three years before the beginning of the fiscal year in which the loss is incurred.

7.16.4 For capital gains tax purposes, any year of assessment in which the property is let as furnished holiday accommodation (or would be, except only for the fact it was being repaired or subject to construction works) is treated as a year in which it is wholly used in the trade.

8 Capital gains tax and your home

Your home is a capital asset so it is potentially the subject of capital gains tax ('CGT'). CGT was introduced into the tax system in 1965 and from its introduction there have been special rules and arrangements which relate to 'private residences'. These rules generally have the effect of eliminating (or substantially reducing) any charge to CGT.

8.1 CGT is a tax on capital gains and is charged at a flat rate of 30% on such gains. Apart from the special relief for private residences there is a general relief for the first £5,600 of gains you make in each fiscal year. For this purpose married couples who have not been separated for a whole fiscal year, are counted as one person.

8.2 What you should do when you buy your home

When you purchase your home, you should tell the Inspector of Taxes of the acquisition by completing the appropriate section of your income tax return. The appropriate section is the section which asks for details of 'chargeable assets acquired'.

If, throughout its period of ownership your home is your 'principal private residence', then you will not have to pay capital gains tax on any profit you make when you sell it. However, if your home is not your principal private residence throughout its period of ownership, then you may be liable to pay CGT on any gain which you make when you sell it. Thus the necessity of recording details of the cost of its acquisition.

The same applies to any money you spend on improving (as opposed to maintaining) it (see 14.14). This will increase its cost and hence reduce any profit which you make when you sell it. It is always very helpful to keep a record of any money you spend on acquiring or improving any property which you own.

You should remember that when you purchase or sell a property your solicitor is obliged by law to inform the Inland Revenue anyway.

The rules relating to whether or not your home can be claimed as your principal private residence are set out next.

8.3 What is your 'principal private residence'? *(CGTA, s.101)*

If you buy your own home, or an interest in it, then for so long as it is your 'main residence' you will not be chargeable to CGT when you sell it. There is no limit to the amount which you can receive free of CGT. Your home may include a garden for this purpose provided the house and the garden do not amount to more than one acre in total. If your house and garden together comprise more than one acre then if you claim, with justification, that the plot is 'required for the reasonable enjoyment of the house, having regard to the size and character of the house', to that extent you will be exempted from CGT on the sale of the land. Otherwise land in excess of one acre (or such larger plot as may be agreed) will not be treated as part of your 'principal private residence' and you may be chargeable to CGT on the sale of the excess land whether with or without your house. There is no territorial limit which restricts this exemption to homes within the United Kingdom.

8.4 Warning note *(CGTA, s.103)*

Before explaining the special rules for your own home, it is worth pointing out that you may not claim the benefit of these rules if the real reason you bought your home was not to live there but to enjoy this special exemption, even though you did in fact live there. For an example of how this might arise, see 8.43.

8.5 Selling a part of your home

If your home is too large and you divide it, selling a part only, or you wish to sell part of your garden, then such a sale is treated as a sale of part of your main residence and is free of CGT. You must be careful, however, if you sell your house and your garden separately, that you exchange an unconditional contract for the sale of your garden *before* you sell the house. If you sell your house first, then the garden which remains is not part of a house any longer, so that a later gain on disposal of the garden might be chargeable to CGT if you sell for more than current use value (see 11.10).

8.6 If you own more than one property *(CGTA, s.101)*

What if you have two homes? Perhaps you own a little cottage in the country and a house in the town where you work. The rule is that only one of these can be your main residence at a time.

The rule for determining which of the two is your main residence is as follows.

From the date (see 8.16) you acquire your second home, you have two years to tell the Inspector of Taxes which of the two is your main residence. You can choose which one it is—so long as it is a *home* in which you do actually live, then there is no special rule which says, for example, you must choose the home in which you spend the most time. Your choice is binding and determines the question definitively if and only if you give

notice of it in writing to your Inspector of Taxes within the two
years from the date of purchase.

8.7   If you have not chosen within two years of the date you
acquire your second home which of the two is your main
residence, then your Inspector of Taxes may decide for you, and
his decision will be based on which of the two is factually your
main home. If you do not agree with his decision you may appeal
to the Commissioners, but they will have to decide on the facts
before them which home is in fact your main residence.

If you own more than two homes, then only one can be your
main residence, and the rule for deciding which one is your main
residence is exactly the same as if you have two homes.

8.8   Even after you have given notice to your Inspector of
Taxes or he has ruled, if you did not decide, which of two (or
more) homes is your main residence, you may, by a fresh notice
at any time, decide which of your homes is to be your main
residence. That notice, which again must be in writing, may be
effective from a date not more than two years *before* the date you
give it. This can be a very useful tax-planning procedure.

8.9   *(CGTA, s.102)*

When you sell your home the question of whether or not you
occupied it in the two years before you sell it is ignored, if the
property has been your sole or main residence all the time from
when you acquired it up to a day not more than two years before
you dispose of it. If you have two homes, you may be able to take
advantage of this rule.

**8.10   Using the CGT rules to your advantage with
two homes**

Suppose you purchase a holiday home for £20,000 in April
1980. You elected then to treat your existing home, which you

bought in 1970, as your main residence. On 1 June 1984 you exchange contracts to sell your main residence and buy another. On 4 June 1984 you elect that with effect from 5 June 1982 your holiday home is your sole or main residence. On 30 May 1986 you elect that with effect from 1 June 1984 your *new* house is your sole or main residence.

The result of these two elections is that for the two years from 5 June 1982 to 1 June 1984 your holiday home is treated as your sole or main residence *but this does not affect* your claim to exemption from a charge to CGT on the sale of your home on 1 June 1984 or a future sale of the home you bought on that day.

8.11 Example 8A

The advantage of the two elections is shown as follows. You sell your holiday home in April 1988 for £30,000. If you did *not* make the elections your CGT is calculated as follows:

	£	£
Sale proceeds		30,000
Less:		
Cost	20,000	
Indexation relief (see 8.37), say,	2,000	
		22,000
Gain chargeable to CGT		8,000

With the two elections the chargeable gain is reduced as follows:

$$\frac{\text{period not occupied as principal private residence (6 years)}}{\text{total period of ownership (8 years)}} \times 8000$$

Chargeable to CGT	=	£6,000
Saving: (£8,000 − £6,000) × 30%	=	£600

8.12 It would be possible (but see below) further to reduce the gain by making a further election in April 1988 on the sale of your holiday home that from April 1986 your holiday home was again your main residence, so giving a total period of four years during which it is treated as your principal private residence. The saving in tax would then be:

$$\frac{\text{period not occupied as principal private residence (4 years)}}{\text{total period of ownership (8 years)}} \times 8000$$

Chargeable to CGT	=	£4,000
Saving: (£8,000 – £4,000) × 30%	=	£1,200

8.13 If the election on the sale of your holiday home mentioned in 8.12 is made, then your other home clearly is not your main home for CGT purposes during that period. This could give rise to a charge to CGT when ultimately you sell that home on the ground that it was not throughout your period of ownership your sole or main home — see the rules in 8.15. If the home you bought in 1984 has risen in value substantially when you sell your *holiday* home, you may consider that the risk of a substantial future charge to CGT when you sell that property would outweigh the benefits of a saving of tax now on the sale of your holiday home.

8.14   Rented accommodation and CGT

If you live in a rented property, and purchase a second property, then you have two places which are your residence. The fact that you live in one as rented accommodation but have purchased the other one does not prevent both places being potentially your 'sole or main residence' for the purposes of CGT. If you do live in rented accommodation and buy another property in which you live, you still should consider which of the two will be your 'main residence' for the purposes of CGT, and make the appropriate election.

8.15 When you may have to pay CGT on selling your home

If a home is *not* for the whole of the time you own it wholly your principal private residence, then you may be chargeable to CGT on a gain you make on its disposal.

8.16 How do you determine exactly when you acquire your home?

Since most of the calculations of how CGT is to be assessed are concerned with time, it is important first to establish exactly when you acquire and when you dispose of your home.

There are a number of ways in which you might acquire your home, and the rules for establishing exactly when you acquired it are as follows.

8.16.1 *(CGTA, s.27)* If you buy your home ready built, whether new or second hand, then you will be treated as having acquired it on the day your contract to buy it has become unconditional. Note that the date you actually pay for your home (completion) is *not* a significant date. In most cases the relevant date is the date you exchange contracts, but if the contract has a condition in it, then the relevant date is the date the condition is satisfied. A condition might be if the contract was subject to planning permission being granted for you to build a garage — in which case the date of acquisition for CGT would be the date that planning permission was granted. A condition which either the buyer or the seller alone can satisfy would be ignored, i.e., a condition that the seller would leave the premises. If the condition was that the contract was conditional on vacant possession, and there was a tenant in the property at the date of contract, the relevant date would be when that tenant left.

8.16.2 *(CGTA, s.49)* You might inherit a house under a will.

If the house was left to you as a specific bequest, then you will be
treated as having acquired the house at the date of death of the
testator — not the date the house was actually transferred to
you. The same would be true if you were left, say, half
somebody's estate, and the executors and you agreed that your
half interest would include that house.

8.16.3 *(CGTA, ss.54 and 55)* You might acquire a house
from a trust of which you are a beneficiary. If you have not lived
in the house while it was owned by the trustees, and the house
becomes yours because, say, you have reached some age, say 21,
specified in the trust, then the relevant date is your 21st
birthday, however long the trustees might take transferring the
house to you. Similarly, if you become the owner of the house
because a life tenant has died, it is the date of the life tenant's
death which is relevant.

8.16.4 Example 8B Your father died on 7 July 1960. Under
the terms of his will your mother was entitled to live in the
family home as long as she lived, and then you were to inherit it.
Your mother died on 30 November 1973. That is the date you
acquire the house, even though you had a reversionary interest
in it from the date your father died.

8.17 When do you dispose of your home? *(CGTA,
ss.20 and 111)*

The rules for determining when a house is disposed of are
broadly equivalent to those on acquisition, with some additions.
(If your house is, for example, destroyed by fire, then the
relevant date is the date you receive the insurance money, but if
you spend the proceeds to rebuild or, within 12 months, replace
your home, receipt of the insurance money is not treated as a
disposal.) If the local authority seeks to acquire your home (say
for a road improvement scheme) under compulsory purchase
powers then the relevant date of disposal is:

(a)   If acquired under a contract, the date of that contract.
(b)   If the authority exercises its powers to enter into the land before compensation is agreed, then the date of entry into the land.
(c)   If agreed earlier than the date of entry under the exercise of its powers, the date the local authority and you agree what the compensation is to be.

8.18   What expenses may you take into account in calculating your capital gains?   *(CGTA, s.32)*

The expenses which you may deduct from what you receive from the sale of your home are as follows:

(a)   What you paid to purchase your home in the first place (or its value when you acquired it, say, under a will or by gift).
(b)   The incidental costs of acquisition, e.g., stamp duty, legal fees, survey costs.
(c)   Any expenditure wholly and exclusively incurred in enhancing the value of the property and which was reflected in the state of the property when sold, such as: double glazing, new central heating, an extension, a swimming pool. However, routine repairs during the time you own the property may not be taken into account. If, when you bought your home, it was dilapidated, you can include whatever you spent immediately after you bought the house in putting it right.

If you have put in an improvement but subsequently removed it, then the cost of the initial improvement will be ignored. (Perhaps you dug a swimming-pool, found it was more trouble then it was worth and then filled it in again. The cost of digging it must be ignored.)
(d)   Incidental costs of disposal, e.g., estate agents' fees or auctioneers' costs, legal costs, costs of advertising, accountants' or valuers' costs reasonably incurred in making valuations or apportioning costs for the purposes

of calculating your chargeable gains.

(e) Costs you incur in establishing, preserving or defending your title to your home. Examples of this might be the legal costs of a dispute with a neighbour concerning a boundary between your properties or the costs of paying compensation to a controlled tenant to persuade him to leave a part of your home so that you could occupy the whole.

8.19 Computation of CGT on sale of your home *(CGTA, s.101)*

If you do not occupy your home as your only or main residence during all the time it is in your possession, then when it is sold you may have to pay CGT on a proportion of the gain which you make. This could arise if you let your home during part of the time you owned it or you might have a second home for part of the time and claim (see 8.6) that the 'second home' was your main residence in that period.

There could, of course, also be other reasons why your home was not your main residence all the time that you owned it and in some of these circumstances it will still be treated for CGT purposes (but not necessarily for income tax purposes) as if it were, so it is worth looking at these circumstances before continuing further.

8.20 Periods which are ignored for CGT when you sell your home *(CGTA, s.102)*

As has been explained in paragraph 8.9 above one such period is a period of time not exceeding 24 months immediately prior to the date of sale (see 8.17).

8.21   Apart from that period the other periods which may be taken into consideration as if they were periods when the property was your only or your main residence, are as follows:

(a)   Any period of time not exceeding three years or any periods of time which, taken together, do not exceed three years.
(b)   Any period when you are required, as a result of your employment or office, to work wholly outside the United Kingdom; or
(c)   Any period of time not exceeding four years during which your employer reasonably requires you to live elsewhere.

These three qualifying periods of absence are treated for CGT as if during them you were actually occupying that home as your only or main residence and may be added to one another.

Considering whether a period falls within any of these exemptions, the question of whether the home was let or empty during the period concerned is ignored. (See also 8.47.)

8.22   If the property is occupied by a dependent relative (see 2.12) then the same exemptions are available so far as concerns that dependent relative as would be available to you, except that any periods during which the dependent relative had some other home available would not be treated as part of the period when the property is a 'principal private residence'. In the case of a married couple, only one home occupied by a dependent relative can rank for this relief at any time.

8.23   *(ESC D4)*

In order for any of the periods of exemption described in 8.21 to apply, it is necessary that *both before and after the period* you live in the property as your only or main residence. There is, however, one relaxation to this rule. If you are unable to resume residence in your home because the terms of your employment require you to work elsewhere, then the period ending with the

date of sale will be included as a qualifying period (provided, if
you move within the UK, it is not longer than either the three-
year period or the four-year period mentioned above).

8.24   Calculation of CGT payable

If a property which has been your home is not your only or main
residence, or the period of ownership does not fall within the
qualifying exemptions set out above, then the proportion of the
period of ownership not falling within the exemption may be
chargeable to CGT.

If the property was purchased after 6 April 1965, then a fraction
of the total gain made will be chargeable to CGT. The period
when the property is not either your main home or treated as
your main home will be divided by the total period of ownership
and the resulting fraction applied to the gain which is made.
CGT will then be payable on the result.

8.25   If you acquired your home before 6 April 1965
(CGTA, sch.5, para.11)

There are special rules which apply if you acquired the property
before 6 April 1965. Then you may choose within two years
after the end of the fiscal year in which you sell your home one of
two alternative bases for calculating what part of the total gain is
brought into the above calculation. If you make no such choice
then the rule is that the gain which you make on the disposal of
the property is treated as having arisen evenly from the date the
property was acquired by you (or 6 April 1945, if later) and the
date the property is sold. The proportion of the gain represented
by the period of time after 6 April 1965 divided by the total
period of ownership will then be applied to the gain actually
made, and that proportion will potentially be chargeable to
CGT.

8.25.1 Example 8C You inherited your parents' retirement home in Devon on the death of your widowed mother on 5 June 1955. At that date the value for probate purposes was £1,500 which, for CGT purposes, is treated as your cost of acquisition. You keep the house as a holiday home, owning another home which is your principal private residence.

On 5 October 1984 the house is sold for £32,100, and you pay fees totalling £1,150 in connection with the sale to your solicitor and the estate agent who found the purchaser.

The CGT payable on the sale is calculated as follows:

	£	£
Sale proceeds		32,100
Less: Sale expenses		1,150
		30,950
Cost of acquisition	1,500	
Indexation relief	200	
		1,700
Total gain		29,250

How much of this gain is chargeable to CGT?

Total period of ownership 5 June 1955 to 5 October 1984
= 29 years 3 months
of which:
Period from 5 June 1955 to 5 April 1965 = 9 years 9 months
Period from 6 April 1965 to 5 October 1984= 19 years 6 months

Proportion of gain chargeable to CGT:

$$\frac{19 \text{ years } 6 \text{ months}}{29 \text{ years } 3 \text{ months}} = \frac{234 \text{ months}}{351 \text{ months}} \times £29,250 = £19,500$$

If you had no other chargeable gains in the tax year 1984/85 the CGT payable on the sale would be:

$(£19,500 - £5,600) \times 30\% = £4,170$

8.26 1965 valuation as an alternative basis *(CGTA, sch.5, para.12)*

The alternative basis, which you may choose within the two-year time-limit mentioned above, is that the property can be valued as at 6 April 1965. Whatever that value might be, the increase in values since that date will be the chargeable gain. Once you choose this option (in the Revenue's terms 'make this election') you cannot subsequently change your mind.

You should be very circumspect before making an election of this sort if your property has increased substantially in value; it is wise to take advice from a qualified surveyor who is experienced in valuations of property in the district where your home is located. The valuation will have to be agreed with the District Valuer and you cannot arrange to find out before you make your choice what figure he will fix.

8.26.1 *Example 8D* In example 8C above, you establish that at 6 April 1965 the value of the property in Devon was £9,000. If you elect that the value at that date is to be used, how would the chargeable gain be calculated?

	£	£
Sale proceeds		32,100
Less: Sale expenses		1,150
		30,950
Value at 6 April 1965	9,000	
Indexation relief	1,200	
		10,200
Chargeable gain		20,750

On the basis of this calculation, the election, if made, would be to your disadvantage; the figure chargeable to CGT is greater by £20,750 – £19,500, i.e., £1,250 than with time apportionment.

8.27 If you acquired your home before 6 April 1965 at a time when its cost or value was very small and have subsequently carried out improvements, then special rules may apply (see 14.15).

8.28 Homes sold for development *(CGTA, sch. 5, para. 9)*

If, when you sell your home, the consideration exceeds the 'current use value' (see 11.10) then there is no option about which basis of valuation is to be used; in these circumstances you must find out what the property was worth as at 6 April 1965 and this will be treated as your acquisition cost for CGT.

8.29 What happens if part of your home is occupied by a lodger?

The special rules for income tax in relation to the letting of part of your home while you live there are explained in 7.3. If you have a lodger living with you as a member of your family, and he shares accommodation with and takes meals with you, then no part of the accommodation will be treated as not occupied as your main residence, and no restriction will apply. The property will be treated as always having been wholly your main residence.

8.30 There are, however, two other circumstances which may have a bearing on potential capital gains tax:

(a) You may let a proportion of your home (say one room out of six) for a lengthy period of time; or

(b)   you may let your whole home for a fraction of the period
       you own it in each year — perhaps you go away for a
       lengthy summer holiday and let your home during the
       period of absence each year in summer.

8.31   How will your CGT be affected by letting your home during the period when you live there?

If you let accommodation in your home so that the part let
ceases to be used as your only or main residence, then the
exemptions to CGT available to you because your home is your
'only or main residence' will be restricted. The extent of the
restriction hangs on two things:

(a)   How much of your home has been let.
(b)   The length of time for which it was let.

8.31.1   *Example 8E*   Suppose, for example, that you bought
your home on 5 April 1970. You wish to sell it on 5 April 1985.
You will have owned your home for 15 years. For nine years you
occupied the home with only your own family living there. For
six years you let three rooms out of the total of eight rooms in the
house. On those facts the proportion of any gain you make on
the sale which will be chargeable to tax will be:

$$\frac{\text{period during which property is not entirely your own home (6 years)}}{\text{total period of ownership (15 years)}} \times \begin{array}{c}\text{proportion of home let}\\ \text{(3 rooms} \div \text{8 rooms)}\end{array}$$

The fraction of the gain chargeable would then be:

$$\frac{6}{15} \times \frac{3}{8} = \frac{3}{20} \text{ or } 15\%$$

so that 15% of the gain would be potentially chargeable to CGT
while 85% would be treated as exempt as the gain made while the

home was your sole or main residence. If the resultant chargeable gain was less than £20,000, no CGT would be payable (see 8.33).

8.32 If you regularly let a part of your home then the calculation will be straightforward.

8.32.1 *Example 8F* In example 8E above, suppose that you let your entire home for 13 weeks each year, i.e., the summer months during which you travel elsewhere. During the period your home is let you keep two rooms to yourself in case you wish to move back to the house. You keep your own personal effects in these rooms. Note that you can argue that the two rooms which you retain whilst the property is let remain part of your 'principal private residence'.

In such a case the proportion of the house which would potentially be chargeable to capital gains tax would be reduced by the periods mentioned in 8.9 and 8.21(a). (You cannot claim this relief in example 8.31.1 because for the last six years of ownership you did not occupy the three let rooms. You could have claimed these reliefs if you had re-occupied the let rooms before you sold the property.)

Period of ownership: 15 years of which treated as wholly occupied — last two years of ownership (8.9)

Balance 13 years, i.e.   676 weeks
of which occupied wholly by you:

39 weeks × 13 years   = 507 weeks
Periods ignored totalling 3 years
(8.21(a))   = 156 weeks

     663 weeks

Balance   13 weeks

Proportion of total gain chargeable to CGT =

$$\frac{13 \text{ weeks}}{676 \text{ weeks}} \times \frac{\text{Number of rooms let in each year (6)}}{\text{Number of rooms available for letting (8)}} = 1.44\%$$

Since you would still be entitled to the £20,000 exemption mentioned in 8.33 the example illustrates how the various reliefs for CGT in relation to your home may together eliminate what would otherwise be a chargeable gain.

8.33   Special exemption for owner-occupiers
(FA 1980, s.80; SP 14/80)

If after 5 April 1980 you sell your home and it has been let during the periods you have occupied it, then the gain calculated above may be exempt from tax.

There is a special exemption for owner-occupiers which applies if the part of your home which you let is an integral part of your home. This would extend, for example, to gains which would otherwise be chargeable to CGT because you have let one or more rooms within your own home. It would not apply in two cases:

(a)   If there was a separate identifiable part of your home which was a dwelling house, for example a granny flat.

(b)   If you had a second house which is capable of occupation entirely separately. (Perhaps you have a large house with a garden and there is a small gardener's house which can be let separately.)

8.34   The special exemption which applies for an owner-occupier is that regardless of whether or not other gains have been made in the tax year, gains which would otherwise have been chargeable to CGT on a disposal of your home will be left out of account to the extent that they do not exceed either (a) £20,000 or (b) that part of the gain which is *not* chargeable to tax by reason of the home being, for the rest of the period of occupation, your sole or main residence. (The maximum exemption was £10,000 from 6 April 1980 to 5 April 1983.)

Even if you make some minor alterations to your home so as to give yourself some greater privacy, if the part you divide off is not a completely separate dwelling-place, then the Inland Revenue will accept that you are entitled to this special exemption.

8.35 In any event, no CGT will be payable if the total gains which you make in any one fiscal year do not exceed £5,600. This exemption is, of course, available to any individual who sells a home which has not been his sole or main place of residence during his period of ownership. If a proportion of your home is occupied in connection with your work, then the rules which are explained in Chapter 17 will apply to that proportion of the gain which you make.

8.36 As explained in 8.18, in calculating the amount of the chargeable gain, certain costs of acquisition and improvement are taken into account and deducted from the proceeds of the sale in order to compute the amount of the total gain realised on the disposal of the property.

8.37 Indexation relief

For sales after 6 April 1982 you are further entitled to increase each of these items of expense by an indexation allowance, provided the expense was incurred at least 12 months before the sale. The indexation allowance is given only for increases in the cost-of-living index after 6 April 1982, and must be applied to the *original* cost incurred.

8.38   How is the indexation allowance calculated?

(a)   For money expended before 6 April 1982. The Retail
      Prices Index (RPI) for each month is published by the
      Department of Employment. The following fraction
      should be calculated:

$$\frac{\text{RPI month of sale} - \text{RPI March 1982}}{\text{RPI March 1982}}$$

This fraction is then applied to each item of expenditure
incurred *before* 6 April 1982 and the result is then added to
the expenditure before computing the chargeable gain.

(b)   If you have acquired your home after 6 April 1982, or
      added or improved it since that date (Chapter 14), then the
      calculation explained in (a) above is adapted by applying in
      the formula set out in (a) above not the Retail Prices Index
      for March 1982, but the Retail Prices Index for the month
      12 months after the month in which the expenditure was
      incurred. (If you disposed of your home before 6 April
      1983, and incurred any expenditure in the 12 months
      ended 6 April 1982, then this rule will be applied as well to
      such expenditure.)

The fraction then becomes:

$$\frac{\text{RPI month of sale} - \text{RPI 12 months after date of expenditure}}{\text{RPI 12 months after date of expenditure}}$$

The resultant fraction is then applied to each item of
expenditure incurred and the result is added to the item of
expenditure as an allowable expense in computing your
capital gain.

If your home was purchased before 6 April 1965 (see 8.25)
then indexation relief is added before the computation of

the gain which has accrued since April 1965. If, therefore, calculation of the gain is on the basis of time apportionment, the indexation allowance must be added to the original cost before computing the gain deemed to have accrued over the period of ownership. If, on the other hand, your home is to be valued as at 6 April 1965, then that value is treated as if it were the expenditure to which indexation allowance is to be added in the computation.

8.39 What are the overall effects of indexation allowance?

The introduction of indexation allowance has been of considerable benefit to those people who purchase a second or holiday home. If you bought such a home after 6 April 1982, and its value has increased only in line with the Retail Prices Index, the profit which you make on its disposal will be, in practical terms, exempted from CGT (except for the 12-month delay in applying the Retail Prices Index). The decision which must be taken, if you do buy a second home, about which home is your principal residence may well be influenced by the dates on which the two homes were acquired. The indexation allowance applies only to the *cost* of your home if purchased before 6 April 1982, even if it was bought 20 years before. If, however, your home was purchased after 6 April 1982 then, apart from the 12-month delay, you may take the full benefit of subsequent increases in the RPI.

If you buy a holiday home after 6 April 1982, it is therefore probably wise to ensure that the home which you purchased before that date, which perhaps was your principal private residence, is the one which you claim to be your 'sole or main residence' (see 8.3). If, on the other hand, you are of the view that the value of the second home which you have purchased is likely to increase very much faster than the Retail Prices Index, then this guideline will not apply.

8.40   The indexation allowance can never serve to reduce a cost or to create an allowable CGT loss. If, therefore, the value of your second home has increased less than the RPI over the period of its ownership, the result will be that you will be treated as having neither made a gain nor a loss for CGT purposes on its disposal.

8.41   Time sharing

In recent years the purchase of a 'time share' in a holiday property has become a very popular way of securing a holiday home. How will the acquisition and ownership of such a holiday home be treated for tax purposes?

8.41.1   Income tax   In order for interest paid on the acquisition of a home to be allowable for tax, remember that it is necessary for the property to be *factually* your 'main residence'. It seems unlikely that you could claim that a time-shared home was your 'main residence'. Therefore interest paid on money borrowed to acquire it would be unlikely to be allowed as a deductible expense by the Inspector of Taxes.

It may be that your time share is three weeks in each year. Suppose in one year you do not take up your three weeks. You may 'swap' your time share with some other person who has the same three weeks in some other time-sharing property. There would be no tax consequences on such an exchange.

What happens if you rent out to some other person the right to occupy your time share? The income which you receive will be taxable as rent in your hands (Chapter 7) and you will be able to deduct all of the outgoings in connection with your ownership of the time share with the exception of any interest which you may pay on money which you have borrowed to acquire it. Even if every year during the period you own the time share you let it out to others, you will not fall within the '26-week rule' (see 7.14) or within the 'principal private residence rule' (explained in 2.1) which are necessary in order to obtain tax relief on interest paid.

8.41.2 Capital gains tax Because the rules for capital gains tax are less stringent than those for income tax, you could technically claim that your interest in a property represented by time share was your principal private residence, and this might be worth doing if it was the only interest in property which you owned, particularly if you are a tenant and rent the home you live in for the rest of the year.

Provided you in fact occupy your time share during the three weeks (in this example) of each year during which you are entitled to occupy it, you could theoretically claim that during the entire period of ownership your time share (which is an interest in land with a dwelling-house on it) is your 'only or main residence'.

Before making such a claim it would be worth considering, however, whether you will in fact make a profit if you sold your time share. If you feel you might make a loss on selling it, it would be worthwhile not claiming that it was your main residence because the loss which you would make on sale would not be an allowable loss if you had previously claimed that it was your main residence. The rules for allowable losses for capital gains tax are the mirror image of the rules for chargeable gains.

8.42 Sitting tenant and CGT (*CGTA, s.103*)

If you are a sitting tenant so that you have the protection of the Rent Act 1977, then if your landlord sold the property (with you as its sitting tenant) he would obtain very much less than its vacant possession value. In such cases it is quite common for the landlord to approach the tenant (or vice versa) with a view to the tenant buying either the freehold (if the property is a house) or a long leasehold interest (if the property is a flat) from the landlord. The price which you will agree with the landlord is usually at a substantial discount on the vacant possession value.

Such a purchase from your landlord is treated both for income tax and for capital gains tax purposes as the acquisition of your home, and the interest which you might pay on money borrowed to buy your home from your landlord (whether freehold or long leasehold) will be treated exactly as if you had bought the property otherwise than as a sitting tenant.

For capital gains tax purposes, however, your Inspector of Taxes will wish to see what you do with the property immediately after you buy it from your landlord.

Suppose, for example, you live in a flat the vacant possession value of which is £60,000 and you agree with your landlord that you may purchase it (by his granting you a long lease at a ground rent) from him for £40,000.

8.43   You may see this as an opportunity to raise £20,000 by selling the flat, and using the £20,000 which you realise in order to put a deposit down on a house.

8.44   If you do sell the property immediately having bought it as a sitting tenant, then your Inspector of Taxes may argue that the profit which you make is not exempt from capital gains tax. His reasoning would be that you have bought your interest in the property 'wholly or partly for the purpose of realising a gain from the disposal if it'. If the Inspector can succeed in this argument, you would not be entitled to exemption from CGT on the profit even though the property is your principal private residence.

The question to be asked is how much of the gain which you have realised from the interest in the property which you have acquired is 'attributable to any expenditure incurred after the beginning of the period of ownership and which you have incurred wholly or partly for the purpose of realising the gain from the disposal'. It is only that part of the gain which can be charged to CGT.

In order to ascertain this you have to go back to the negotiations you had with your landlord. Your landlord has sold you the property for £40,000 instead of the vacant possession value, i.e., £60,000, because you are already occupying the property.

8.45 Instead of selling the property to you for £40,000, your landlord might have paid you a sum in consideration of which you agree to give up your protection as a sitting tenant. Suppose that he would have paid you £12,000 to leave, so that he could now realise £60,000 by selling the property with vacant possession. If your landlord pays you money to leave the property in which you live, then the amount which you receive will not be chargeable to capital gains tax so long as the property in which you have been living has been your sole or main residence throughout the period you have lived in it.

The chargeable gain which you realise by buying the property for £40,000 from him and selling it for £60,000 yourself is, however, only the difference between the gain you realise from buying and selling again, i.e., £20,000, and what you would have received from the landlord even if you had not bought the property from him but instead had vacated, i.e., £12,000.

The difference between these two figures, i.e., £8,000, is potentially chargeable to capital gains tax but *not* the whole of the profit which you make.

8.46 Job-related accommodation *(CGTA, s.101(8); ESC D3)*

If you occupy job-related accommodation (see 2.17) and purchase another home with the *intention* of its becoming your sole or main residence, then even if you do not occupy it during the years after 30 July 1978, any such periods are treated as if they were periods during which it is your sole or main residence, and so to that extent you will be exempt from CGT in respect of any gains you may make on the sale of the property, even if it has been let throughout your period of ownership (see also 16.17).

It is not a requirement that you do in fact so occupy the property; you must satisfy the Inspector of Taxes that it was your intention to occupy it. Any evidence you can produce will be helpful, for example, correspondence with your solicitor or the agents acting on behalf of the vendors. Very good evidence might be the terms under which you let the property (if you do): for example, if you include a specific provision dealing with your right to require tenants to vacate if you are posted home.

This rule also applies if you own a property but your spouse lives in job-related accommodation.

8.47   CGT and your home after your death
  (ESC D5)

The rules which gave exemption from CGT for your home cease at your death. Your personal representatives are treated for CGT as if *they* had acquired your home at its value on the day you died. If, under the provisions of your will, an individual inherits your home, then he or she is treated as having acquired your home at the date of death and at its then value, so that in those circumstances the personal representatives are not concerned with CGT.

It may be, however, that after your death your personal representatives will continue to hold your house for some time, either because your will provides that they should or because it takes them some time to sell the house.

8.48 In these circumstances, the following rules apply:

(a) If, both before and after your death, the property was the main home of an individual who is entitled to inherit the whole, or the greater part, of its value, or to occupy the property during his or her lifetime, then the personal representatives will be exempt from CGT when they sell the property.

(b) In any other circumstances, the personal representatives are chargeable to CGT on the full gain which has arisen since death and do not enjoy the exempt amount to which an individual would be entitled. If, however, the gain arises to the personal representatives in the fiscal year in which you die or the next two fiscal years, they are given the same £5,600 annual exemption as an individual.

8.49 Homes owned by trustees *(CGTA s. 104)*

If your home is owned by trustees, and you occupy it under a provision of the trust which allows you to do so, then the trustees will enjoy the same reliefs in respect of your home as you would have enjoyed if you yourself had owned it. If you have two homes, one of which is owned by trustees, then the choice (see 8.6) of which home is entitled to relief must be determined by an election signed jointly by you and the trustees.

8.50 If, under your will or during your lifetime, you establish a trust, then the trustees of that trust are given half the exempt amount an individual might enjoy (or a fraction of that half if during your lifetime you created settlements which continue at the time of the sale). The most common form of a settlement under a will is a provision that an individual may live in a house or enjoy an income for his or her lifetime or until he or she marries.

9 Capital transfer tax

If wealth leaves you because of an action by you (such as a gift), or on your death, a tax known as capital transfer tax (CTT) is charged. The tax is chargeable *not* on the value of what the recipient of your wealth receives, but on how much poorer you are after making the gift or transfer than you were before it was made. Since their home is for most people the largest part of their wealth, it is often the asset which is most relevant for CTT purposes. Many of the rules which apply to calculate this tax differ from the rules for other taxes, and they must be considered separately. As explained in 9.10 there is, however, a close relationship on certain occasions between capital gains tax (CGT) and CTT.

9.1 When is CTT payable? *(CTTA, s. 2)*

Certain gifts are exempt from CTT (see 9.2). Apart from such exempt gifts CTT is payable whenever a transfer of value (see 9.3) is made. All such transfers of value made during your lifetime after 26 March 1974 are added together to find out what rate of tax applies to each latest gift or transfer of value. Gifts made during your lifetime are also added to the value of your assets which pass at the date of your death to establish what additional tax, if any, is then payable.

There are two important exceptions to this general rule.

(a) Any transfer between a husband and wife, or the passing of assets on death to the surviving spouse, is wholly exempted from all the calculations and from CTT unless the

Table 9.1

Cumulative chargeable transfers (gross) £	Rate on gross %	CTT on band £	Cumulative CTT £	Cumulative chargeable transfers (net) £	Rate on net
DEATH RATES					
0 – 64,000	Nil	Nil	Nil	0 – 64,000	Nil
64,001 – 85,000	30	6,300	6,300	64,000 – 78,700	$\frac{3}{7}$
85,001 – 116,000	35	10,850	17,150	78,700 – 98,850	$\frac{7}{13}$
116,001 – 148,000	40	12,800	29,950	98,850 – 118,050	$\frac{2}{3}$
148,001 – 185,000	45	16,650	46,600	118,050 – 138,400	$\frac{9}{11}$
185,001 – 232,000	50	23,500	70,100	138,400 – 161,900	1
232,001 – 285,000	55	29,150	99,250	161,900 – 185,750	$1\frac{2}{9}$
285,001 +	60			185,750 +	$1\frac{1}{2}$
LIFETIME RATES					
0 – 64,000	Nil	Nil	Nil	0 – 64,000	• Nil
64,001 – 85,000	15	3,150	3,150	64,000 – 81,850	$\frac{3}{17}$
85,001 – 116,000	$17\frac{1}{2}$	5,425	8,575	81,850 – 107,425	$\frac{7}{33}$
116,001 – 148,000	20	6,400	14,975	107,425 – 133,025	$\frac{1}{4}$
148,001 – 185,000	$22\frac{1}{2}$	8,325	23,300	133,025 – 161,700	$\frac{9}{31}$
185,001 – 232,000	25	11,750	35,050	161,700 – 196,950	$\frac{1}{3}$
232,001 – 285,000	$27\frac{1}{2}$	14,575	49,625	196,950 – 235,375	$\frac{11}{29}$
285,001 +	30			235,375 +	$\frac{3}{7}$

transferor is domiciled within the United Kingdom and the spouse is domiciled elsewhere (CTTA, s. 18(2)).

(b) Ten years after the transfer it is excluded from future calculation of the total of transfers of value taken into consideration (CTTA, s. 7).

9.1.1 *Rates of CTT* CTT is charged at the rates shown in Table 9.1.

The higher scale is applied if you die within three years of the chargeable transfer of value.

9.2 Exempt gifts *(CTTA, ss. 19-26)*

Certain gifts, if made during your lifetime, are wholly exempted from capital transfer tax. These are as follows:

(a) In each fiscal year you may make gifts up to £3,000 to any individual or individuals and such gifts will be exempt from tax. If you give more than £3,000 but in the immediately preceding year gave less than £3,000, then you may increase the amount of this year's exemption by the amount by which your gifts last year were less than £3,000.

(b) You may give to each of as many individuals as you wish an amount not exceeding £250. An individual who has received part of the £3,000 mentioned in (a) above may not also receive such a gift of £250.

(c) In addition to the two exemptions set out above, a gift which is part of 'normal expenditure out of income' may be exempt from capital transfer tax. In order to be exempt the gift must satisfy all of the following three criteria:

(i) It must be a gift which is regular. A gift each year on your birthday might be regular, particularly if you sent a letter with the first gift saying you intended to make an equivalent gift each year on your birthday, (or on the recipient's birthday).

(ii) The gift must be out of your after-tax income. If you are non-domiciled (see 13.3) then income for this purpose would include income which arose to you outside the United Kingdom and which had not been taxed here because it had not been remitted here. For this purpose the term 'income' excludes money you receive from an annuity which you apply to pay premiums on a life insurance policy associated with the annuity policy.

(iii) The gift must be such that it does not reduce your usual standard of living.

(d) Gifts or legacies to charities are exempt from capital transfer tax without limit.

(e) Certain gifts in consideration of marriage not exceeding £5,000 if the donor is a parent of one of the marriage partners are exempt; the figure is £2,500 for a gift from a grandparent or great-grandparent or from one of the parties themselves. In any other case a gift of £1,000 will be exempt. The exemptions apply to gifts in respect of each marriage whether the gift is made to one of the partners in the marriage or to a settlement in favour of the partners and their children.

(f) Gifts for national purposes or for the public benefit. If you give your home, for example, to the National Trust or the National Heritage Memorial Fund, then such a gift would be wholly exempt from capital transfer tax. The same would be true of gifts generally for the public benefit — if the Treasury agree.

9.3 What is a 'transfer of value'? *(CTTA, s. 3)*

CTT during lifetime is calculated by reference to the loss of value of your total assets (your 'estate') which follows on a voluntary action which you take. It is not necessarily equal to the value which is received by the person who benefits from your voluntary action. CTT is payable in the normal course of events by the person who makes the gift. The consequence is that CTT is paid not on the value of what is given but on a larger figure. The larger figure is calculated to be such a sum as includes the tax on it.

9.3.1 *Example 9A*

In 1984/85 you have already made gifts which absorb your annual exemption (see 9.2.1). Since 26 March 1974 you have made no other gifts chargeable to CTT. You give your house, worth £100,000, outright to your son. This is treated as a gift of £107,000 to your son because the CTT on a gift of £107,000 is exactly £7,000. You are treated as having made a gift to your son of a house plus tax of £7,000 because as a result of the gift you are poorer by the loss to you of the value of the house, i.e., £100,000, and your liability to CTT as a consequence of the gift, i.e., £7,000.

If as an alternative to your paying the CTT, you agree with the person to whom you make a gift that that person will pay the tax then the 'grossing-up' procedure explained above will not apply. As a result of your gift you are poorer only by the value of the house that you have given.

9.4   Interests in trusts   *(CTTA, ss. 51 and 52)*

Another example of a 'transfer of value' would be if you ceased to have an 'interest in possession' in a trust. This might happen if you were the life tenant of a trust created by your mother's will and as such were entitled, until you yourself married, to live in the house which she had previously owned. Perhaps under her will after your marriage your younger brother will become entitled to live in the house. On the occasion of your marriage, the trustees would be treated as if, on your behalf, they had made a transfer of value of the entire house. Any tax liability as a consequence would fall on them, but the value of the house would be taken into consideration when calculating your own cumulative total for CTT in respect of any future transfers of value which you yourself might make.

There are several more complicated circumstances in connection with trusts which might give rise to a transfer of value, but consideration of such technical matters, other than in respect of homes, is beyond the scope of this book. The exemption for gifts between husbands and wives (see 9.1.1) would extend to an interest under a trust so that if on your ceasing to be entitled to live in a house your spouse would be entitled to live there (perhaps your widow on your death) then this would not be treated as a transfer of a value at your death.

9.5 You can see that in certain circumstances a transfer of value which may affect your future liability may take place 'over your head'.

9.5.1 Example 9B An illustration of the way in which this could arise would be the following.

Mr Longarm provides under his will that his widow may live in the family home rent-free until she remarries and on her death it will pass to his son. If she remarries the home will then pass to his son immediately. Mr Longarm dies and Mrs Longarm, his widow, lives in the family home. There is no transfer of value on Mr Longarm's death because on his death his home is being occupied by his widow.

Some years later Mrs Longarm meets Mr Spritely whom she marries. On the day she marries Mr Spritely, Mr Longarm's old home was worth £100,000. Because Mr Spritely had his own home, Mrs Longarm was not very worried about the fact she could no longer live in her previous home and she is quite pleased that it now goes to her son.

She is quite well off because of other funds which she has and decides that on marrying Mr Spritely she would like to make a gift to her daughter. She works out that she has not made any gifts in the previous tax year so that she has total exemptions for possible gift to her daughter of £6,000 (see 9.2.1). She knows that she may make gifts totalling £64,000 on which no tax would be payable and calculates that if she makes gifts of £70,000 to her daughter this would not give rise to a charge to tax now. She draws a cheque on her bank and pays £70,000 to her daughter. She is told that she must make a return of the non-exempt part of the gift which she understands is £64,000 (£70,000 – exempt gift £6,000) and she completes the appropriate return.

She is horrified when she receives an assessment to capital transfer tax of £11,645 as a result of the gift which she made to her daughter. How has this happened? What Mrs Spritely did not take into consideration when she made the gift to her daughter was that she was treated as having already made a transfer of value on her marriage to Mr Spritely. Under the terms of her previous husband's will, she was no longer entitled to live rent-free in the former family home. She was therefore treated as having made a transfer of value of the entire market value of the house. Indeed the trustees of her late husband's will would have had to pay some capital transfer tax. Her liability on the gift to her daughter is calculated as follows:

	£	£
Transfer by trustees		100,000
Transfer to daughter	70,000	
Less: Exempt	6,000	
		64,000
		164,000
Add: CTT on gift to daughter		11,645
Total on which CTT is payable		175,645

How was the charge to CTT which Mrs Spritely received worked out?

	£
Tax on transfer by trustees of £100,000	5,950
Tax payable on lifetime transfers of £175,645	17,595
Balance payable by Mrs Spritely	11,645

If Mrs Spritely had died within three years of the gift to her daugher, the figure would be doubled.

If you are entitled to live in a home under the terms, for example, of somebody's will and if you then cease to be entitled to live in it (or die) that event will be a transfer of value and part of your cumulative total (see 9.1).

9.6 Homes within discretionary trusts: transfers of value *(SP 10/79)*

If the trustees of a trust are empowered to allow a beneficiary to live in a house, and they exercise this power and permit a beneficiary to occupy a dwelling-house, then, even though the beneficiary does not have a life tenancy, the Inland Revenue will consider the terms under which that permission is given. If, say, the beneficiary is one of several people who may live in the house at the same time (perhaps a flat by the seaside to which many beneficiaries may go to live for a few weeks at a time) then this will be ignored. If the trustees create a contractual tenancy for full consideration then again this will be ignored because it is an ordinary commercial transaction.

There are, however, some circumstances which the Inland Revenue might consider would give rise to a charge or a potential future charge to CTT.

The trustees may grant you a lease to your home at below market rent for a fixed term or a periodic tenancy. This will be treated as a gift to you by the trustees (and will not in fact affect your CTT cumulation). The main problem, however, is likely to arise if the trustees grant you the right to live in a home (either exclusively, or jointly with somebody else) so that effectively that place becomes your permanent home. Once such an arrangement comes into existence the *ending of it will be treated as a transfer of value*. It might end for a number of reasons. For example:

(a) You might die while still living there.
(b) The trustees might exercise a power to bring your right to live there to an end.
(c) The right might have been given for a fixed period of years and not be renewed.

Any of these events in connection with your home would affect *your* cumulative total for CTT. It would not make any difference if you had another home as well.

9.7   How is your home valued for CTT?

On a transfer of your home during your lifetime or at your death, in order to calculate the CTT which might be payable on the transfer, your home must be valued. The value will be established by the District Valuer, who will have a record of all transactions in properties in your neighbourhood, and to whom your transfer will be submitted by the Capital Taxes Office (the section of the Inland Revenue responsible for the administration of CTT). The District Valuer will not be bound by any figure which you or your advisers propose.

9.8   As a general rule if within two years of the transfer of value, the property which was the subject of the gift or the legacy has been sold, then the gross sale value will probably be substituted by the District Valuer for whatever figure was originally proposed. It may be that within the period of two years a major change has taken place making such a sale value inappropriate. An obvious example might be if on the date your mother died and left you her home, there was a sitting tenant. At the date of her death the house, with a sitting tenant, was worth, say, £40,000. A year later, after the house has been transferred by the executors to you the sitting tenant leaves. You now, within two years of your mother's death, sell the house for £70,000. Although that sale has taken place within two years of the death, you may argue that the value at date of death must take into consideration the depressed value because there was a sitting tenant. The District Valuer would accept this argument although he may not necessarily accept that the figure which was first put forward, i.e., £40,000, is the correct one. (Note, you may well be chargeable to *CGT* on the difference between the agreed value at the date of your mother's death and the *net* sale proceeds.)

9.9   If a house which has, for example, been left to you by will is sold within two years, then as explained above the value for CTT will be revised as at the date you inherited it to the gross value of what you received for it when you sold it. It is improbable that when you sell the house you will not incur any selling costs such as legal fees and estate agents' fees but these are not deductible in calculating the value of the property for CTT purposes (although they are deductible for the purposes of CGT).

9.10   *(CGTA, s. 49(4))*

As explained in 8.47, the personal representative who owns a home will in most cases be liable to CGT when he disposes of it. What happens therefore if executors sell a house within two years of death and the District Valuer insists that the sale value must be taken to be the value at the date of death? Suppose the sale value of a house at the date of death was £90,000 and the selling costs were £3,000. If the executors sell the house they will be treated as having made a £3,000 loss for CGT purposes. They may not be able to enjoy any relief for this loss. If the house has been left to a beneficiary it would be a far better idea if

the executors transferred the house to the beneficiary (who will
be treated as having inherited it at the date of death) and he or
she then sells the house. This will make no difference for CTT
purposes but the loss for CGT purposes will now accrue directly
to the beneficiary and may be made use of by him (where the
home is not his main residence) either in that year or in future
years.

9.11 Joint ownership of homes

There are a number of circumstances in which more than one
person may own one home. Mention of the way in which
interest relief may have been given to joint owners is explained
in 3.9. For the purposes of CTT it is first important to find out
on what basis a home is jointly owned. The most common form
of joint ownership is probably where a husband and wife buy a
house together in which they then live. There are certain
circumstances in which a house, although registered in the name
of only one party to a marriage, may as a matter of law belong to
both of them. A common circumstance might be if, for example,
a house were bought in the name of a husband but the wife
contributed substantially to the cost of acquisition of the home.
This particular aspect of joint ownership forms part of
matrimonial law as well as of property law and is outside the
scope of the present volume.

9.12   There are two ways in which individuals might jointly
own a home, and they have different legal and therefore possibly
taxation consequences:

(a) They may be joint tenants.
(b) They may be tenants in common (either in equal or
     unequal parts).

Put simply a joint tenancy is an arrangement by which on the death of one of the joint tenants, the property, the subject of the joint tenancy, passes automatically to the survivor (but not necessarily in Scotland).

The alternative way in which two people might own a property together is if they are 'tenants in common' and in this case each party has his or her own share in the property, which he or she may dispose of how they think fit. The interests do not pass by survivorship.

Either party to a 'joint tenancy' may 'sever' the joint tenancy after which the tenancy becomes a 'tenancy in common' which may be in equal or unequal shares.

9.12.1 Example 9C Mr Brown provided in his will that on his death his home should pass to his two unmarried sisters, Angela and Caroline. The house is registered in the joint name of Angela and Caroline. Angela makes a will under which she leaves all her estate to her nephew, Tom. When Angela dies, Caroline is still alive and lives in the house which had been left to her and to her deceased sister by her late brother, Mr Brown. Tom is very disappointed when he finds that he has not received the half-share in the house because it has passed by survivorship to Caroline.

He is even less happy when he discovers what the consequence is from a tax point of view.

On Angela's death the house is valued at £105,263. Angela on her death owned a half-share and the District Valuer agrees that because Caroline was living there and had the right to live there a 5% discount from market value would be appropriate for her half-share. Angela's half-share was therefore valued for CTT purposes at £50,000. Angela's estate, other than her interest in the joint house, was worth £60,000 but her total estate, for capital transfer tax purposes, will be treated as being £110,000. The capital transfer tax on an estate of £110,000 is £15,050 and

Tom now has to pay his share of that. His share is calculated as £15,050 × £60,000/(£50,000 + £60,000), i.e., £8,209. Caroline of course has to pay her share which is £15,050 × £50,000/(£50,000 + £60,000), i.e., £6,841, but, as explained in 9.18, she has 10 years during which she may pay this tax by 10 annual instalments. Interest will run on the instalments as explained in 9.18 at a rate of 6%.

If, during her lifetime, however, Angela had severed the joint tenancy with Caroline so that they had re-registered their interests as tenants in common — in this particular case in equal parts — then under the terms of Angela's will, Tom would have inherited not only the £60,000 which he received as explained above, but also half the house in which Caroline lived. He would of course have had to pay all the tax, and would have had the same rights to pay by instalments as Caroline had in the example set out above.

Incidentally, if in the second example Tom, who now owns a half share in the property, allows Caroline, who is old or infirm, to live in the house without paying rent, then as she, too, is his aunt she will be a 'dependent relative' (see 2.11) and Tom will not have to pay CGT if, when he sells his half share in the house, it has doubled in value.

This example has left out a number of practical questions such as what happens if Tom wants to sell his half share in the house.

9.12.2   *Example 9D*   In example 9C, a completely different set of circumstances might arise if, after her brother's death, Angela marries. It is then very important that Angela considers whether to sever the previous joint tenancy with Caroline. If she does, then she may leave her half share in the house to her new husband. Because this is a transfer to a surviving spouse, it is exempt from CTT. If she has not severed the joint tenancy then, on Angela's death the half share will revert to Caroline, who may find she will have a charge to capital transfer tax on inheriting

Angela's previous half share by survivorship.

If you are the joint owner of the property, and you are not sure of
the basis upon which you are the joint owner, do talk to your
solicitor and establish precisely the basis on which your joint
ownership is recorded. Your and your family's tax liabilities
may be affected by the answer. It is a relatively simple
procedure to 'sever' a joint tenancy and your solicitor will be
able to advise you on the procedure.

9.13   Valuation of jointly owned property

When any asset is to be valued for the purposes of CTT it must
be valued at the price which it would fetch in the open market. If
what is owned is an interest in joint property then the open
market value of such an interest will be less than the equivalent
proportion of the whole. If, for example, a property is owned as
joint tenants, each is assumed to have a half share but a
deduction of 5% would generally be acceptable. If the joint
ownership is more complicated, for example, a tenancy in
common or perhaps a joint right to occupy a property under the
provisions of a trust, then a discount from vacant possession
value of 10% may be accepted by the District Valuer. The
discount applied will not increase merely because your interest
in a tenancy in common is less than 50%. If, for example, you
owned a one-quarter share in a property jointly with your two
brothers and sister, then your share of the property would be
valued as 25% of the value of the whole property less a discount
of 10%. The Inland Revenue will not agree that a greater
discount than 10% is appropriate.

9.14   Homes, farms and businesses   *(CTTA, ss. 103–114, 169)*

Under the general rules for valuation for capital transfer tax,
there are several provisions under which only a proportion of

the value of an asset needs to be brought into account in calculating capital transfer tax. In some circumstances your home may be given the benefit of these provisions.

In order to enjoy this benefit it would be necessary to show that your home was an asset of, or used in, some business, trade, profession or occupation which you conducted. Examples of this might be if your home was a cottage or farmhouse occupied with your farm and of a character appropriate to the property. In such a case the farm as a whole would rank for agricultural relief, and only 50% of its value would be taken into consideration in calculating a transfer of value of which the farm formed part. If your home is a farmhouse, you are therefore entitled, in considering capital transfer tax, to the same relief in respect of your home as you are entitled to in respect of the rest of your farm. If you own an agricultural cottage occupied by a farm worker, the cottage is valued ignoring any higher value it might have to someone else without such an occupier.

9.15   If you have retired as a farmer but still live in what was formerly the farmhouse, you may find that the Capital Taxes office will seek to deny this relief in respect of your home. This might arise, for example, if a new farmhouse were constructed on the farm and occupied by your son and from which in practical terms he then conducted the farming activities.

9.16   Another circumstance in which the same relief of 50% might be given would be if you 'live over the shop'. Perhaps you have bought a shop with a flat over or you are a doctor who uses one room of your house exclusively as a surgery (but see 16.9).

In such cases the whole building is valued and the proportion of it which is used for business purposes is reduced by 50% in calculating the total value to be taken into consideration for the purposes of CTT.

In cases where either business relief or agricultural relief is claimed, the relief is given only if the person making the transfer of value has owned the relevant asset for at least two years before the event. This rule may be relaxed if there are two transfers of value within the two-year period.

There is a further limitation to these reliefs and that is that any liabilities associated with the asset must be deducted before the relief is due. If you have bought your farm (including your farmhouse) with the help of a mortgage, then that mortgage must be deducted from the value of the farm in order to calculate the figure on which relief may be given.

9.17 Exempt gifts and your home

There are a number of schemes which have been suggested by which you may give slices of your home to your family, taking advantage of the exemptions mentioned in 9.2(a) and (c). These schemes are mostly somewhat artificial. The legislation in relation to capital transfer tax specifically provides that artificial arrangements of this sort may be nullified, and if you are minded to enter into this sort of arrangement you are advised to take legal advice concerning the efficacy of the arrangements before entering into them.

9.18 When is CTT payable? *(CTTA, ss. 226, 227)*

CTT is payable when as a consequence of a transfer of value the total of chargeable transfers reaches such a level that it exceeds £64,000. The relevant tables showing the calculation of tax are set out in 9.1.1. In the normal course of events such tax will be payable six months after the relevant transfer of value; in the case of a lifetime transfer made after 5 April and 1 October in any year, the tax is payable 30 April in the next year. If the tax is paid late then interest will run on the amount of any tax paid late at a rate of 8% per annum in the event of the gift made during lifetime, or 6% per annum if the tax payable is a result of a transfer on death.

9.18.1 If on your death a charge to CTT has arisen on the value of your home, then your executors may claim to pay the CTT attributable to your home by instalments. These instalments would run for 10 years and would be payable as 10 annual instalments. Unless your home ranked as agricultural property or ranked for business relief (see 9.14) interest would be payable in respect of the instalments calculated from the original date. If your home ranks for agricultural or business relief, interest runs in respect only of an instalment paid later than the due date of that instalment.

9.18.2 If you have made a gift of your home during your lifetime, and the person to whom you have given it agrees to pay the CTT, then the right to pay the tax by instalments is extended to a lifetime gift with the same interest provisions explained above.

9.19 International aspect *(CTTA, s. 267)*

If you are domiciled within the United Kingdom at the date of a transfer of value, then it does not matter where your asset is located, the transfer will give rise to a charge to capital transfer tax. There are special rules, however, under which certain individuals may be treated only for the purposes of CTT *as if they were domiciled in the United Kingdom even though they were not in fact domiciled there.* Such a domicile is usually known as 'deemed domicile'. It will come into effect if you have been resident for income tax purposes (see 12.3) within the United Kingdom in at least 17 of the last 20 years before the relevant event. In practical terms once you have been resident for at least 16 years, you will be deemed domiciled on the first day of the 17th fiscal year.

9.19.1 Example 9E You were born in Italy of an Italian

father and have been sent by your Italian employers to manage their British subsidiary. You came to Britain on 1 April 1969 and have been resident in Britain continuously since that date. You will be deemed domiciled in England (if that is where you have been living) with effect from 6 April 1985.

Explanation. You were first resident for income tax purposes in the tax year 1968/69. 1984/85 was therefore the 16th year in which you were resident for income tax purposes. 6 April 1985 is the first day of your 17th year of income tax residence. From that date on you will be 'deemed domiciled' in England and would therefore be subject to capital transfer tax in respect of your worldwide assets.

9.20 There is one important exception to this rule which relates to your home. For the purpose of determining whether you are resident for income tax purposes, you may ignore any year in which you are treated as resident *only* because of the availability of accommodation in Britain (see 12.3.3).

9.21 If you are domiciled or 'deemed domiciled' at any time within three years of the date of the relevant transfer of value, then you will still be deemed to be domiciled as at that date.

If you are neither domiciled nor deemed domiciled within the United Kingdom, then you will be subject to capital transfer tax only in respect of transfers of assets which are 'within' the United Kingdom. If your own home is within the United Kingdom, therefore, you would be subject to capital transfer tax if you, for example, died owning your property and it was not inherited by your spouse.

If you are domiciled within the United Kingdom but your spouse is not, then the exemption for transfers between spouses will not apply to you. If, for example (after 1 January 1974) you married a Frenchman who comes to live with you in your home in London, then if you leave your home to him in your will, the CTT payable on your death would be the same as if he were not married to you. If he had acquired a domicile of choice in Britain (see 13.5), then this rule would not apply.

9.22 A problem which may arise if you are not domiciled within the United Kingdom would be if you are posted from abroad for a few years and you wish to purchase an expensive home within the United Kingdom during the years you are working here. Because your home is in the United Kingdom, it will form part of your 'estate' for CTT purposes. If you are not married then on your death substantial CTT would be payable when your home devolved; the same would apply if you were married and you and your wife died simultaneously — for instance, in a travelling accident. If, however, the house is owned by a foreign body corporate, then the asset which you own is the shares in the foreign body corporate rather than the house, and therefore not located within the United Kingdom. Although such a transaction will be effective for CTT purposes, it has the disadvantage that it may bring on to you a substantial charge to income tax because of the provisions for calculating benefits (see 10.2 to 10.7). If these circumstances are likely to affect you it is important to take advice from an accountant or solicitor versed in these particular questions.

9.23 *(FA 1984, s. 121)*

If you are no longer resident in the United Kingdom (see 12.2) when you sell your home, or it is owned by an overseas company, there may be a DLT problem if the property is sold after 5 August 1984 (see 11.18).

10   Your employer and your home

10.1   Benefits

If your employer provides you with your home or pays any expenses in connection with it, then generally you will be subject to income tax on the benefits which you enjoy. There are some special cases in which you may not have to pay tax on benefits, and rules to measure how much the benefit is.

10.2   The value of your benefits   *(FA 1977, s. 33; FA 1983, s. 21)*

If you occupy a home made available to you by your employer (or somebody else who provides the home *because* of your employment) then you will be subject to tax on *the value of the accommodation provided*. This is measured as the 'annual value' of the property less any rent you pay to occupy the home. In practice the 'annual value' is equal to the gross rateable value (see 17.7).

10.3   An additional income tax charge will arise in 1984/85 and subsequent fiscal years if, when purchased by your employer, such a home cost more than £75,000 (or, if it was purchased by your employer more than six years before you occupied it and you first occupied it after 30 March 1983, then if its market value *when you first occupy it* exceeds £75,000). A further charge to income tax calculated at present at 12% of the excess of cost (or value as explained above) over £75,000 will be added to the benefits (if any) described in the previous paragraph. This would mean that even if you pay your employer rent equal to or even exceeding the property's gross annual value, you would be subject to this additional tax charge, less such excess.

10.3.1 *Example 10A* On 1 January 1982 your employer provides you with a home which costs him £100,000. The gross rateable value of the property is £1,250. As part of the terms of the occupation you make a contribution to the costs (by way of rent paid to your employer) of £1,000 p.a.

In 1984/85 your taxable benefit will be calculated as follows:

	£
Gross rateable value	1,250
[(Cost of property £100,000) – £75,000] × 12%	3,000
	4,250
Less: Rent paid	1,000
Taxable benefit	3,250

10.4 There are some extra rules which apply to this additional tax charge. If there is any business use of the property the expense of such use may be deducted in calculating the benefit. If your employer spends money on improving the property, then the costs of such improvements would be added to the original cost or market value at the date of occupation.

The substitution of market value for cost will only apply if your employer has owned *an* interest in the property for at least six years continuously before you occupy it.

10.4.1 *Example 10B* On 5 April 1974 your employer purchased a 21-year lease of a home in London for £5,000. On 5 April 1982 he purchased the freehold for £50,000. You are provided with the use of the house rent free on 5 April 1983. On that day the value of the house was estimated (on the basis of the price it might reasonably be expected to fetch in the open market, assuming vacant possession and disregarding any option in respect of the property held by you or your employer) at £100,000. Your employer has held *an* interest in the property for more than six years, so you will be taxed on a benefit equal in value to the gross annual value *plus*:

$$(£100,000 - £75,000) \times 12\% = £3,000$$

If the gross annual value is, say, £1,000, your taxable benefit would be £4,000 p.a., which figure is added to your earned income in calculating your income tax liability.

10.5 Other benefits *(FA 1976, s. 63)*

If you are a director *or* higher-paid employee (over £8,500 p.a.) then if your employer pays other expenses relating to the house for you then the cost of these would be added to your taxable benefits to the extent that you did not reimburse him. Examples of such expenses would be:

(a) Rates.
(b) Heating costs.
(c) Lighting.
(d) Garden maintenance.
(e) Domestic or other services.
(f) Interior repairs or decoration.
(g) Insurance.

10.6 Not included in such expenses would be:

(a) Ground rent paid by your employer.
(b) External repairs.
(c) Improvements (but see 10.4).
(d) Service charges in a block of flats (or a proportion of them if they include non-allowable items such as heating).
(e) Repairs, water, gas, electrical or water or sanitation or heating installations.

10.7   Furniture supplied by your employer in your home   *(FA 1976, s. 63; FA 1980, s. 49)*

In addition, if furniture or other contents are provided by the employer then 20% of the cost to the employer would be added to these benefits; this would apply even though you owned your home yourself (in which case the benefits in 10.2 and 10.3 would, of course, not arise).

10.8   Representative occupation   *(FA 1977, s. 33(4))*

There are certain circumstances in which none of the above charges to tax will apply unless you are a person to whom the rules explained in 10.10 below apply. You will not be charged to tax on the benefit of a home provided by your employer if:

(a)   It is necessary for the proper performance of your duties that you reside in the accommodation (if, say, you are a caretaker); or

(b)   The accommodation is provided for the better performance of your duties and your employment is one of the kinds for which it is customary for employers to provide accommodation for employees (if you are, for example, a bank manager or a publican living on the premises); or

(c)   There is a special threat to your security, special security arrangements are in force and you reside in the accommodation as part of these arrangements (for example, you live in police housing).

10.9   Occupation under such circumstances is termed 'representative occupation' or 'job-related occupation'.

The exemption extends to any tax charge that would otherwise be made because of rates paid on behalf of or reimbursed to you.

10.10 Directors or higher-paid employees in representative occupations *(FA 1977, s. 34)*

If you are the director of the company or an associated company, the exemptions in 10.8 do not apply to you, even to the limited extent explained below, unless:

(a) You have no 'material interest' in the company (by which the Inspector of Taxes means that you and your associates hold less than 5% of the company); and

(b) You are a 'full-time working director' *or* the company is recognised as a charity *or* the company does not carry on a trade *or* the company's functions do not consist wholly or mainly in the holding of investments or other property.

Directors or higher-paid employees are entitled only to some of the reliefs if they fall within the categories of representative occupation set out in 10.10 above. The taxable benefit in respect of additional services set out in 10.5 and 10.7 is reduced in respect of:

(a) Heating, lighting or cleaning of the premises concerned.

(b) Repairs to the premises, their maintenance or decoration.

(c) The provision in the premises of furniture, etc., which is normal for domestic occupation.

In respect of *these items* the sum on which you might be taxed will not exceed 10% of your income from the employment but that figure would be further reduced by any contribution you make to those expenses. These restrictions are not applied if you are entitled to representative occupation on security grounds.

10.11 General exclusions

There are two other circumstances in which you will not be charged to tax in respect of a home provided to you by reason of your employment:

(a) If your employer is an individual and your home is provided in the normal course of his domestic family or personal relationships.

(b) If you are employed by a local authority and you occupy a council home on the usual terms such homes are provided by the authority to people living there who are not local authority employees.

10.12 Loans by your employer *(FA 1976, sch. 8; F(No. 2)A 1983, s. 4)*

If your employer, or somebody connected with him, has lent you money either interest free or at a low rate of interest, generally you would be charged to tax on the benefit of the saving in interest such a loan gives you. The notional rate of interest on which you would be taxed is 12%.

If, however, the loan was to help you buy your house or it replaces another loan which you had for that purpose, then you may be exempt in whole or in part from such a charge.

If the total of your mortgage from, say, the building society (if you have such a loan) and from your employer does not exceed £30,000, then no charge to tax will be made. If, however, you *do* borrow from your employer a sum which, together with other loans, exceeds £30,000 to purchase or improve a house then you will be charged to income tax on 12% of the excess of such borrowings over £30,000. For this purpose, any interest-free loans which you may have *not from your employer* (say from a member of your family) which you used to acquire or improve your home must be included in the total.

10.12.1 Example 10C On 1 July 1980 you borrowed £25,000 from the building society to buy a house for £50,000. On 5 April 1984 you borrowed £15,000 interest free from your employer to build an extension to the house. In 1984/85 the

building society charges you interest at 10% gross on your mortgage.

The total interest you would be *deemed* to pay would be:

	£
£25,000 @ 10% to the building society	2,500
£15,000 @ 12% to your employer	1,800
	4,300

The maximum borrowing on which you could have claimed exemption was £30,000 so you would be taxed on a benefit of:

$$(£40,000 - £30,000) \times 12\%, \text{ i.e., } £1,200 \text{ in } 1984/85$$

10.13 Moving expenses paid by your employer *(ESC A5(a))*

If you are a director or higher-paid employee you will not be charged to tax on benefits enjoyed by you because your employer pays your removal expenses. This exemption will apply if:

(a) You have to move to take up new employment; or
(b) Your employer transfers you to another post within his organisation.

The expenses must be reasonable in amount and they must be properly controlled.

10.14 The sort of costs which might be included would be:

(a) Agents' fees for selling your old house.
(b) Legal fees or expenses on the sale of your old house and the purchase of your new house, including stamp duty and

initial costs for a new mortgage other than any mortgage guarantee premium.

(c)   Furniture removal and storage costs.

(d)   A contribution of a proportion of the cost of fitting carpets and curtains in your new house, and costs of alterations to existing loose furnishings moved, or a general allowance towards these expenses not exceeding, say, 5% of your salary.

(e)   Temporary subsistence allowance or hotel accommodation costs while you look for a new home, and for your family for a limited period during the move.

(f)   The reimbursement of interest costs on a bridging loan (net of tax relief) or a bridging loan from your employer tax free (within the £30,000 limit explained in 2.9) for 12 months or longer if you can persuade the tax authorities that a longer period is justified.

(g)   An undertaking that your employer will purchase your previous home at the end of, say, six months at forced-sale value if you have been unable to sell it for at least that figure.

(h)   If you have paid club fees or other expenses such as church dues or school fees which you cannot use because you have to move, reimbursement of such wasted expenditure.

10.15   The Inland Revenue may allow some further assistance by an employer with the cost of financing a move, particularly if a group of employees are requested to relocate in new facilities, when the move is from an area where housing costs are low to one where they are high — say, from Newcastle to London.

The form of such further assistance could be either a loan at low (or nil) interest or an interest-rate subsidy, which must taper over, say, five years. The restrictions which would apply to such assistance are as follows:

(a)   The accommodation must be equivalent to that from which you moved — not, say, a move from a two-bedroom terraced house to a four-bedroom detached house.

(b) The subsidy must be restricted to reimbursing outgoings of a revenue nature such as rent, rates, ground rent, mortgage interest, etc. and not items of a capital nature such as mortgage loan repayments, cost of house extensions, etc.

(c) The subsidy must only cover the *net* cost of the move to the individuals concerned after taking into account tax saved, for example, on mortgage interest paid.

(d) The payments must taper.

(e) The payments must not be in the form of a lump sum.

(f) There must be a reasonable ceiling on the total of all the payments.

11 Development land tax and your home

Land in the United Kingdom is subject to planning control. If you own land you may not change the use of that land without obtaining planning permission. If you do obtain planning permission the value of the land may increase considerably. Over the years various governments have tried to tax the benefit of obtaining such permission and since 31 July 1976 a tax regime known as 'development land tax' (DLT) has been applied in such cases. As in the case of CGT, there are special exemptions in the case of your home (see 11.12).

11.1 *(DLTA, s. 1)*

The scheme of DLT is that a tax charge at a flat rate of 60% applies on all 'realised development value', with the exception of the first £75,000 of such realised development value which is not charged to DLT (£50,000, if the disposal was before 1 April 1984) for each year ended 31 March.

11.2 The relationship of DLT and CGT *(DLTA, sch. 6)*

As the rules for DLT and CGT are not the same, particularly in defining the occasion of charge, special rules have been laid down to cover their interaction.

11.2.1 *Simultaneous disposals under both taxes* This occurs when land is sold. If DLT is payable, it is paid in full.

The amount chargeable (but not the exempt band of £75,000) is excluded from chargeable gains for CGT purposes and then indexation allowance is given. The deduction of DLT cannot create or enlarge a loss for CGT purposes.

11.2.2 DLT disposal first, CGT disposal second If you commence a project of material development and sell the land afterwards, the DLT is paid at the commencement. The subsequent sale of the land by you would be chargeable to CGT. The amount chargeable to DLT is excluded from the CGT computation as in 11.2.1.

11.2.3 CGT disposal first, DLT disposal second This will arise usually when two people are concerned with the land; the first person transfers land without payment, either by way of a gift or as a transfer to a beneficiary from a settlement to the second person. No charge to DLT arises at that moment but a charge to CGT may, unless a holdover election has been made (see 1.22).

If a charge to CGT has arisen, then the recipient of the land may deduct part of the CGT paid from his subsequent DLT liability on sale or commencement of a project of material development within 12 years of his acquisition of the land.

11.3 When is development value realised? *(DLTA, s. 4 and sch. 2)*

If land is situated within the UK, then a number of events in connection with that land may give rise to a charge to DLT. 'Realised development value' can arise on either the actual realisation of development value or on the happening of a number of events which are treated as a deemed disposal and give rise to a charge to DLT. A deemed disposal occurs when a project of material development (but see 11.11) is commenced. A project of material development commences at the earliest of any of the following events:

(a)   A work of construction in the course of the erection of a building.

(b)   The digging of a trench which is to contain the foundation, or part of the foundations, for building.

(c)   The laying of an underground main or pipe to the foundations.

(d)   Any operation in the course of laying out or constructing a road or part of a road.

(e)   Any operation in the course of winning or working minerals on the land.

(f)   Any change in the use of any land, where that change constitutes material development.

11.4   A change of the use of the land which constitutes development would take place, for example, if after having obtained planning permission, say, to use your home as offices, you commenced to use your home as offices. It will cover any circumstance in which, without there being any change to the physical structure of the land or building standing on it, the actual use of the land is changed following a grant of planning permission to make such a change in its use.

11.5   On what is DLT payable?

DLT is payable on the amount of the chargeable realised development value accruing to the taxpayer in each year ended 31 March (and not 5 April).

11.6   What is realised development value?

This is the surplus of what you receive (or are deemed to receive) on the occasion of the realisation of development value (from which you may deduct the incidental costs of realisation such as stamp duty, legal fees, valuers' costs, etc.) over 'relevant base value'.

Before going on to define 'relevant base value' it may be helpful to keep in mind the object of DLT. It has been expressed as being to obtain for the community a proportion of the value created by the community in the granting of planning permission. In the calculations, therefore, it is necessary to bring in an estimate of what the value of your land or buildings was before the planning permission. 'Relevant base value' is the technical term used by which the legislation brings in this value, with an additional margin of error in favour of the taxpayer.

11.7 How is relevant base value calculated?
(DLTA, s. 5)

The relevant base value is the highest of three possible calculations, base A, base B and base C.

11.7.1 Base A Base A is defined as the total of the following items:

(a) Cost.
(b) Expenditure on 'relevant improvements'.
(c) Any increase in 'current use value' which has arisen after 6 April 1965 or after the date of acquisition, if later.
(d) The special addition.
(e) The further addition.

11.7.2 Base B The total of 115% of the current use value, together with the expenditure on 'relevant improvements'.

11.7.3 Base C The total of 115% of the cost (unless the land concerned was part of a residential development held as trading stock in which case the factor is 150% after 9 March 1981) and 115% of expenditure on improvements.

11.8 *(DLTA, s. 6)*

You will only be concerned with the definitions of special

addition and further addition if you acquired your land or an interest in land before 1 May 1977. If you acquired your land before 13 September 1974 the 'special addition' was 15% of the original cost for every year of ownership up to four so that the maximum would be 60% of the cost. If you acquired your land after 12 September 1974 (still before 1 May 1977) the special addition is limited to 10% of the original cost for each year of ownership up to four, giving a maximum of 40% of the cost. In both cases, a part of the year is treated as a full year.

11.9 If you acquired your land before 1 May 1977 and subsequently carry out any 'relevant improvements' then the 'special addition' above is applied not only to the original cost but also to 'relevant improvements'. This is the 'further addition', calculated as:

$$\text{special addition} \times \frac{\text{relevant improvements}}{\text{original cost}}$$

Relevant improvements consist of those items on which you expend money with a view to enhancing the value of the property or defending your title to it to the extent that they do not increase current use value.

11.10   What is 'current use value'?   *(DLTA, sch. 1)*

The term 'current use value' is applied not only for the purposes of DLT but also for the purposes of CGT (see 8.28). Current use value is the value of your land (or the home which stands on it) on the assumption that it would be unlawful to change the planning use which applies to it. If, therefore, you live in a home with a few acres of land attached to it, and you obtain planning consent to construct houses on the additional land, such planning consent would not change the 'current use value' of the land. If, however, you have already commenced building works then that would in itself have been an occasion of the commencement of a 'project of material development' so that on a subsequent sale of the land the current use value would be the enhanced value of the land with the planning consent for building works on it.

11.11 Development projects which are not material

Certain events will not give rise to a charge to DLT because they are not treated as being 'material'. These are:

(a) Changes of use of the land where the change is *within* one of the following classes:

Class A. A dwelling house or activities not carried on for profit (if your house is used as a chapel or clubhouse for a boys' club such a change would not be 'material').

Class B. Office or retail shop.

Class C. Hotel, boarding house, public house, etc.

Class D. Used for other commercial activities (other than agriculture or forestry) not within any of the other classes.

Class E. Manufacturing, warehousing, etc.

(b) An alteration which does not increase the volume of your home by more than one third.
(c) If you rebuild your home, if the new building does not exceed the volume of the old by more than 10%, and there is no change of use as in (a) above.
(d) If you use your home for agriculture or forestry.
(e) If you use your land for advertising purposes.

11.12 When may you have to pay DLT in connection with your home? *(DLTA, sch. 14)*

Just as in the case of CGT, there are substantial exemptions available to private individuals in connection with their 'principal private residence'. The definition used for the purposes of DLT is exactly the same as that for CGT (see 8.3). If you realised development value from the land falling within the definition of your principal private residence, you will be wholly exempt from DLT if and only if:

(a) You have owned it for at least six months.
(b) It has been your only or main residence:

    (i)   if you have owned it for at least two years, then for at least 12 out of the 24 months before disposal; or
    (ii) if you have owned it for less than two years, then for at least half of that period or for a continuous period of six months whichever is the greater.

If you have used a part of your home exclusively for the purpose of a trade, business or profession (see 16.9) then the realised development value must be apportioned and the exemptions from DLT applying to private residences will apply only to that part of your home which was not used exclusively for the purposes of your trade, etc.

11.13   The exemption is extended to a number of cases other than those when you own your own home:

(a) If your home is owned by a trust and you are entitled under the terms of the trust to occupy it.
(b) If within two years of the death of the occupier the personal representatives dispose of the land.
(c) If the home is occupied rent-free by a dependent relative (see 2.12).

11.14   If you acquired land before 12 September 1974 and subsequently construct a single dwelling on that land, the construction of such a home will be wholly outside the charge to

DLT if the person who is to occupy the home is you or your spouse (or, if you are divorced, your ex-spouse), a dependent relative, an adult member of your family, i.e., son or daughter of you or your spouse aged over 18 (including an adopted, illegitimate or step child), your father or mother or your spouse's father or mother or, if the individual concerned is illegitimate, the natural father or mother of that person.

11.15 Building a home on land acquired after 12 September 1974 *(DLTA, s. 15; FA 1984, s. 119)*

If you bought land after 12 September 1974 and, after 12 September 1974, on that land, commenced the construction of a home at a time when you had full planning permission for the project, then the charge, if any, to DLT may be deferred until you factually dispose of your home, and will be entirely extinguished 12 years after the deemed disposal which gave rise to the deferred charge.

11.16 Additional matters concerning DLT

The £75,000 exemption which has been referred to above applies to each individual so that if the land is owned and developed jointly by husband and wife up to £150,000 of realised development value is exempt.

References in the computation to 'cost' are treated literally. If you have received land by way of gift (or inheritance) you will not have paid anything for the acquisition of the land. The 'cost' which will then apply to you will be the cost of the land to the person from whom you received or inherited the land. This can give rise to anomalies if, for example, you inherited land which had been acquired in the 1930s by your father for £100 and its value for CTT on your father's death was £100,000. For DLT purposes the cost is still £100. In such circumstances it is likely that the use of base A defined in 11.7.1 would not be the most advantageous in computing the charge to DLT on the disposal of the land.

11.17   Other exemptions

11.17.1   Since DLT is a charge related to the grant of planning permission in the United Kingdom, it is never chargeable in relation to land outside the United Kingdom.

11.17.2   A disposal for no consideration, such as the gift of your home or its passing on death, is not an event for DLT purposes, so no charge to DLT arises.

11.17.3   If, within three years of your acquiring land, you commence building works or any of the other actions treated as the commencement of a project of material development, then no further charge to DLT will arise — unless you could not, when you purchased the land, have immediately started the work without a charge to DLT arising then.

11.17.4   If your home is within an enterprise zone then no charge to DLT arises on its sale.

11.18   Sales after 6 August 1984 by non-residents
(DLTA, s. 40; FA 1984, s. 121; SI 1984 No. 1172)

If you are not resident in the United Kingdom when you sell your home, a new rule will apply if the sale takes place after 6 August 1984 so that the purchaser of your home must retain 40% of the sale price and pay it to the Inland Revenue as a deposit against any DLT liability that you might have on the sale. This does not apply if the consideration for your home does not exceed £150,000 (£75,000 if the property sold is not a dwelling).

12 *International aspects*

In today's complicated world of international business many people find that they move from one country to another for periods of years. During this time they may own or occupy homes in several countries and this will have taxation consequences which are sometimes quite unexpected.

12.1 'Resident', 'ordinarily resident' and 'domiciled'

The term 'resident' is a special one used for tax purposes, and whether or not you are a 'resident' of the United Kingdom will have a significant bearing on your taxation liability.

A simple definition of 'resident' might be 'where you would be physically in a fiscal year', whilst 'ordinarily resident' might be 'where you would usually be over a longer period'. 'Domiciled' might be 'where in the long term you intend to live'.

12.2 'Resident' *(ICTA, s. 122)*

If you are resident in the United Kingdom then broadly speaking you will be subject to UK tax on all your income and capital gains arising anywhere in the world. If you are domiciled (see 13.2) elsewhere, then your UK taxation liability will be based on income or capital gains arising *in* the UK together with only that part of the income or capital gains *arising* elsewhere which you *bring* to the UK.

12.3   *(IR20, paras 8–11)*

The Inland Revenue have laid down a series of tests to determine whether you are resident in the United Kingdom and if you meet *any* of these you will be treated as being resident here.

12.3.1   If you spend at least 183 days in any fiscal year physically in the UK you will be treated as resident.

12.3.2   If you are a habitual visitor and spend on average 90 days in each fiscal year in the UK you will be treated as resident. You may ignore in this calculation the days of your arrival or departure.

12.3.3   *(ICTA, s. 50)*   If you maintain a home (technically known as 'available accommodation') (see 12.5) in the UK and set foot for even one day in the UK you will be treated as resident in the fiscal year in which that day falls. The effects of this might be overridden if you are also a resident of some other country with which the UK has a double taxation convention.

12.4   You will also not be treated as resident by virtue only of available accommodation if you are engaged *full time* abroad in a job, whether as an employee or on a self-employed basis. To be accepted as working full time abroad no part of your duties (other than those merely incidental to your job) may be carried out in the UK. The term 'incidental' is not the same as 'insubstantial'. If, for example, you are a portrait painter and live abroad, keeping a *pied-à-terre* in London, then even painting one portrait in a fiscal year in England would be enough in that year to make you a 'resident'.

12.5   What is 'available accommodation'?   *(IR20, para. 28)*

The Inland Revenue explain what they mean by 'available accommodation' as follows:

Where a person's residence position turns on whether or not he has available accommodation, the question is whether any accommodation is in fact available for his use. For this purpose ownership is immaterial — a person does not have to own or rent a house, apartment or other accommodation for it to be available for his use: contrariwise, a house he owns and lets out on a long lease under the terms of which he has no right or permission to stay in it will be ignored. A house owned or rented by one spouse will usually be considered available for the use of the other. But any accommodation rented for use during a temporary stay here may be ignored if the period of renting is less than two years for furnished accommodation or one year for unfurnished accommodation.

The dividing line can be illustrated as follows. The manager of the Grand Majestic Hotel in London says to you, 'We will always have a room for you whenever you come to London'. That is not 'available accommodation'. If, on the other hand, he says, 'We will keep room 1234 just for you', then that *is* 'available accommodation' even though you do not own it.

Because of the importance of this rule for people who take jobs outside the UK, you must be very careful about your home if you intend to leave the UK but return for visits.

If your home is let, then it will be ignored as it is not available to you even if you return. It is not sufficient, however, to stay somewhere else in the UK if you *could* stay in the home you retain; you would still be treated as resident in the UK in that year.

12.6 Husbands and wives *(ICTA, s. 42)*

When a man is offered a job abroad his wife will usually accompany him but she may spend much longer in the UK than he does; she may also stay in the family home in the UK. As she (unlike her husband) is not in full-time employment abroad *she* may therefore be treated as resident in the UK in any fiscal year she comes here. It can be seen that in these circumstances the husband would be 'non-resident' but the wife would be 'resident' in the UK for such a year.

If you are in this situation, and if you could gain from it you may claim to be taxed as if you were not married in that year (see 6.1).

12.7   What happens when you leave the UK?   *(IR20, paras 13–17)*

The taxman will accept that from the day you do leave the UK you are non-resident so long as you do not come back permanently to the UK in that or the following fiscal year. If you leave the UK half-way through the tax year you are still entitled to the whole of your personal allowances for the fiscal year in which you leave so that you should normally be able to reclaim some income tax if you have been subject to PAYE before you leave. In order to find out if you have indeed ceased to be resident the Inspector will ask you to complete a form P85. He will then decide whether and from what date you are non-resident. He will base his decision on the following tests.

12.8   If you claim that you have ceased to be resident and ordinarily resident in the UK and can produce some evidence of this (for example, that you have sold your house in the UK and set up a permanent home abroad) your claim as a non-resident will usually be admitted provisionally with effect from the day following your departure. Normally this provisional ruling is confirmed after you have remained abroad for a period which includes a complete fiscal year and during which any visits to the UK have not amounted to an annual average of three months.

It is not, however, an essential requirement that you stay outside the United Kingdom for a complete fiscal year. If you do not it will take much longer for the Inspector of Taxes to agree that you have become non-resident, although once his agreement has been given it will be given retrospectively to the day on which you left. If you cannot comply with the requirements set out immediately above, the decision will be postponed for three years and would then be made by reference to what actually happened in that period. During the three intervening years, your taxation liability will be computed provisionally on the basis that you remain resident in the UK. You will therefore provisionally be entitled to receive the various income tax personal allowances due to a resident of the UK except for any tax year in which you do not set foot in the UK. Your liability will be adjusted, if necessary, when the final decision is made at the end of three years.

12.9 Employment abroad *(IR20, para. 18)*

These stringent rules will be relaxed if you go abroad under a contract of employment requiring you to work full time abroad. In those circumstances, you will normally be regarded as not resident and not ordinarily resident in the UK from the date of your departure until the day preceding the date of your return, so long as:

(a) The duties of your employment are performed abroad, or any duties you perform here are incidental to your duties abroad;
(b) Your absence from the UK in the employment is for a period which includes a complete tax year; and
(c) You do not visit the UK for more than six months in one tax year or three months or more on average.

12.10 Letting your home

Once you are no longer resident in the UK you will probably want to let your home. It is important before doing so to check with your building society or other lender that they are happy with the terms of the proposed letting. Your mortgage may well restrict your right to let without first obtaining clearance from the lender, who may have the right to increase the interest rate you are charged if you yourself do not occupy the property. (If your interest is paid under the MIRAS scheme — see 3.17 — your lender may insist that your payments are no longer eligible for the scheme so that the interest is paid gross. You will then have to claim the interest as a deduction in your tax computation.)

12.11 Letting your home when you are non-resident   *(ICTA, ss. 54, 70 and 89; ESC B13)*

Once you are non-resident then income tax must be deducted from the net rental income or from the gross rental before you receive it. If the rent is collected by an agent (who might be an estate agent or a friend or relation) then the agent is personally liable to account for income tax to the Inspector of Taxes based on the amounts *he pays to you*. If the tenant pays rent directly to you when you are non-resident the tenant may be directed to deduct tax and pay it directly to the Collector of Taxes; if there are arrears of tax the tenant may even be told to pay the whole rent to the Collector until arrears of tax relating to that letting are made good.

If you are letting through an estate agent he will be assessed to tax in your name, and almost certainly will retain money from the rent he receives to pay the tax when it falls due. If he proposes to do this make sure you agree the terms on which he will hold such funds. If the funds are substantial you should ensure that you enjoy the benefit of any interest which he can earn (although the interest itself will be liable to income tax).

You may be able to arrange that your bank will indemnify the agent for any tax liabilities so long as you keep an equivalent amount on deposit with the bank. This has the advantage while you are non-resident that the interest you earn directly from the bank will not itself be liable to income tax. If you earn interest through an agent this concession will not apply.

12.12 How will the tax be calculated when you are non-resident?

If you are a non-resident you are not subject to UK income tax on your world-wide income, but only on such part of your income as arises in the UK, which would include rent from properties in the UK. The taxation liability on such rent will be the same whether or not your tenant is British or pays you outside the UK or in some currency other than sterling; what governs your liability is where the property is located.

12.13 Personal allowances and non-residents (ICTA, s. 27)

If you are non-resident then you cannot claim to set off all your personal reliefs (such as your personal allowance or married man's allowance) against your rental income but, if you are a British or Irish subject, or a resident of a country which has an appropriate double taxation agreement with the UK, you may claim a proportion of such allowances. The proportion is:

$$\frac{\text{your income liable to tax in the UK}}{\substack{\text{your world-wide income (even if} \\ \text{you are not domiciled in the UK)}}} \times \text{allowances}$$

12.14 If you want to claim such proportion of your allowances, you will have to complete a tax form FR12, on which you will have to disclose to the UK tax authorities the whole of your world-wide income including that part which is not subject to tax in the UK.

Many non-residents do not wish to disclose their world-wide incomes to the British tax authorities — nor are they obliged to;

it is only if they wish to claim a proportion of their personal allowances that this requirement arises.

12.15   Otherwise, non-residents' rental income will be subject to income tax at the rates set out on page 5.

12.15.1 Example 12A   If, in example 7B, the property was let by a non-resident and the notional wear and tear allowance was applied, the position would be:

Schedule D Case VI income	£2,492
Tax thereon @ 30%	£ 747

12.16   Husbands and wives: let property

Sometimes where a husband works full time abroad, his wife will stay in the family home for part of the year, and the house will be let for the rest of the year. Another case might be where the family have, say, a second home in Britain which is let for the whole year, whilst the wife stays in the principal home for part or whole of the year.

In such a case if the property is owned by the wife alone, or jointly by husband and wife, it may pay to claim that although the husband is non-resident, the wife is resident in the UK, as explained in 12.6. The wife would then be subject to income tax on the rental income, but in addition to offsetting mortgage interest paid in connection with the let property (and also any mortgage interest on the principal home if that is separate and additional), she could also, as a resident, set off her own personal allowance without regard to her husband's income. Furthermore, if she was a resident the agent who collected the rent (if there was one) would have no obligation to account for income tax, and so could pay the whole of the rent to the wife without withholding money for tax.

12.16.1 Example 12B In the year ended 5 April 1985 Mr Jones works for the whole year (except for leave of 40 days) in Saudi Arabia where his employer provides accommodation. He and his wife own two properties in Britain. One property is let for the whole year, the net rent being £5,000 p.a., and mortgage interest payable is £2,000. The other property is the family home on which mortgage interest of £1,200 p.a. is payable. The houses are in the joint names of Mr and Mrs Jones. Mr Jones spends a few weeks in the family home in 1984/85. Mr Jones earns £33,000 in Saudi Arabia. Mrs Jones has no other income.

If Mr Jones claims that the let property is his and discloses his Saudi income to claim a proportion of his married man's allowance then he will pay tax as follows:

	£	£
UK income		
Let property		5,000
Less:		
Mortgage interest		
Let property	2,000	
Home*	1,200	
		3,200
Taxable UK income		1,800
Less: Proportion of personal allowances:		

$$\frac{1{,}800}{33{,}000 + 1{,}800} \times £3{,}155 \qquad 163$$

Taxable in UK	1,637

Tax payable in UK as a result of letting home:

£1,637 × 30%	491

*Mr Jones may claim to deduct the mortgage interest which he pays on his own (unlet) home because his home in Saudi Arabia is 'job-related accommodation'.

12.16.2 *Example 12C* If, however, the employment arrangements in Saudi Arabia do not include the provision of a home, the computation is:

	£
	£
Let property	5,000
Less: Mortgage interest	2,000
Taxable UK income	3,000
Less: Proportion of personal allowances:	

$$\frac{3,000}{33,000 + 3,000} \times £3,155 \qquad\qquad 263$$

Taxable in UK	2,737

Tax payable in UK as a result of letting home:

£2,737 × 30%	821

12.16.3 *Example 12D* Alternatively, Mrs Jones claims that she is resident in the UK and receives the income; her tax computation will be as follows:

	£	£
Let property in UK		5,000
Less:		
Mortgage interest on let property	2,000	
Mortgage interest on principal residence	1,200	
		3,200
		1,800
Less: Part of single person's personal allowance (£2,005)		1,800
Taxable UK income		nil

Tax payable: nil

12.17 Interest relief on a home in the United Kingdom when your employer requires you to move elsewhere *(ESC A27)*

The rules which require that a property must factually be your sole or main residence are relaxed if your employer requires you to move elsewhere, whether within the UK or abroad, if your absence is not expected to exceed four years. During that period you may claim tax relief on the mortgage interest you pay whether or not you live in the property.

The concession lasts only four years but starts again once you have lived in the property for a period of three months.

The concession also extends to a property purchased while you are employed abroad, provided during the period you are abroad you live in the property for a period at least three months before you return to become resident.

This concession is an alternative to a claim that interest paid may be deducted from taxable income arising from rents.

13 Visitors from abroad and property abroad

Many individuals who usually live elsewhere may come to the United Kingdom for longer or shorter periods. While they live here they may acquire or live in homes in the United Kingdom and they may retain and let out or sell the homes they had in the country from which they came.

13.1 Residence, ordinary residence, domicile

Mention has already been made in Chapter 12 of the terms 'resident' and 'ordinarily resident', and the rules for establishing when the Inland Revenue think you *become* resident or ordinarily resident in the United Kingdom are explained in 12.3.

13.2 What is domicile? *(IR20, paras 31–4)*

Domicile is a concept of international law, and British tax law looks to your domicile (rather than, say, to your nationality) to establish to what extent your British tax liabilities are affected by events elsewhere.

Your domicile is where you intend to make your permanent home (and not necessarily where you maintain your present home or any previous home). United Kingdom law maintains that at any one time you must have a domicile, and there are a number of procedures which are followed to try to fix this. (This subject is a complex one and these notes are only a brief summary; if you are in doubt you should consult a lawyer or practising accountant experienced in such questions.) If you have a domicile in the United Kingdom it will be English or Scottish or Northern Irish (but not British), although for *tax* purposes these three are equivalent to one another.

Your domicile will be established as one of three types:

(a) Of origin.
(b) Of dependency.
(c) Of choice.

13.3 Each individual is born with a domicile of origin, which is your father's domicile at the time of your birth, and not necessarily the place where you were born.

For example, if your father was in the British diplomatic service and all his connections were with Scotland, but at the time you were born your father was posted to Australia where your mother joined him and where you were born, then your domicile of origin is Scottish and not Australian.

If no other domicile overrides it, the law will always presume that you intend to return to your domicile of origin.

13.4 If, during your minority your father changes his domicile then your domicile will follow that of your father. If he dies or divorces your mother and you stay with her and she changes her domicile, then your domicile will follow that of your mother until you reach your majority when you determine your own domicile. Such a changed domicile during infancy is a domicile of dependency.

Prior to 1 January 1974 a married woman was treated as having a domicile of dependency which was the domicile of her husband, and any woman married before that date retained that domicile afterwards unless she changed it by positive action.

13.5 It may be that you have cut all your links with your country of origin and put down new roots in the UK with the intention of making your permanent home here. In that case you may have given up your domicile of origin and acquired a domicile of choice. It is much easier to give up a domicile of choice than to lose a domicile of origin, which would, for example, revive if you left your adoptive country and did not settle down in a new country.

13.6   How does your domicile affect your UK tax?
(ICTA, s. 122)

If you are not domiciled within the UK, you will not be subject to income tax on any rental income you may receive from your 'overseas' home unless you bring the rent to the UK. In practice, you should not be taxed if you arrange that rent which you receive from your overseas home is banked in a separate bank account outside the UK, and that bank account is not used by you as a source of funds to bring money to the UK or to pay debts which you incur here.

13.7   Interest paid on a mortgage on your overseas home   *(ICTA, s. 181; FA 1974, sch. 2, para. 6; IR25, paras 3.13–18)*

It may be that you keep your overseas home and do not let it, but still pay mortgage interest on money you borrowed to buy it before you came to Britain. It was explained in 2.1 that interest paid in connection with a home outside the UK or the Republic of Ireland was not allowable for tax but there is one exception to that rule.

If you are not domiciled within the UK, and you are seconded to the UK by your overseas employer to work for your employer or a subsidiary company in Britain, your earnings for such work from an overseas company (but *not* from a company resident in the UK) will be 'foreign emoluments'. If your earnings are foreign emoluments, you may ask the Board of Inland Revenue to grant you relief for payments you make abroad corresponding to those which, if made in the UK, would be allowable for tax. Mortgage interest you pay in connection with your overseas home is such a payment; if you make a claim for relief against your UK tax liability for any such interest paid it will be allowed, but you must show that you do not have income outside the UK (except your foreign emoluments) from which you could have paid the interest.

If you are domiciled within the UK you cannot in any circumstances make such a claim.

13.8   Your holiday home abroad

Many people today are tempted to buy an overseas holiday home in, for example, Spain or Florida. You will receive no tax relief at all in connection with such a purchase, and the tax consequences can be very unfortunate if, for example, you let the property at times you are not there.

13.8.1   Perhaps you want to buy a condominium in Florida for £40,000, and the local agent tells you that you can borrow £20,000 at 10% to help finance it and that he can let it for £2,400 a year for the weeks you are not there. The way the figures *appear* are as follows:

	£	£
Rent receivable		2,400
Agent's letting fees	240	
Local taxes	160	
	400	
		400
		2,000
Mortgage interest		2,000
Net annual cost		nil

13.8.2   Unless you are domiciled outside the UK your British Inspector of Taxes will see the figures a bit differently. He will calculate:

	£	£
Rent receivable		2,400
Agent's letting fees	240	
Local taxes	160	
		400
Taxable in the UK		2,000

He will not give you relief for the interest.

If you pay tax at 40%, he will ask for income tax of £800 (= £2,000 × 40%) — an unwelcome surprise. The calculation would be just the same if you borrow the money from your British bank and in whatever currency you borrow.

13.9   If you *do* want to buy a property abroad, and let it out, it might be worthwhile to form a company resident in the UK to buy the property and for that company to borrow the cost from a bank in Britain. A company (but not an individual) will be allowed to deduct mortgage interest from foreign rental income. You would have to pay rent to the company when you stay there but this may be needed to pay the interest. If you do not pay rent you would be taxed on the benefit as calculated in 10.2 to 10.7.

13.10   Practical points

Another point to consider is what would happen if you die owning a property abroad. Your executors may find they have to engage expensive lawyers just to obtain title to your holiday home, and in some countries such as France and Spain there is very high stamp duty on any transfers. If your holiday home is registered in the name of a UK company, no such problems would arise because what you would own is UK assets, i.e., the shares in the company. A simpler solution which may be satisfactory would be to purchase the property in the joint names of you and your spouse (and possibly your adult children) who might inherit by survivorship under local law, so avoiding the necessity to prove a will in the country where you have your holiday home.

If you are considering buying a holiday home abroad make sure you take advice in Britain to see what tax consequences here will be — do not rely on the agents abroad.

Do not forget that there are many local taxes outside Britain some of which are similar to income tax or rates — but some of which are rather different, such as wealth or capital value taxes or taxes on deemed income from your own occupation.

13.11   Foreign currency bank accounts and your holiday home   *(CGTA, s. 135)*

A gain which arises to you because of a profit on a foreign currency bank account, even with a bank in the UK, is usually chargeable to CGT when you withdraw money from the account.

13.11.1   Example 13A   In 1981 you opened a US dollar bank account with $20,000 when the exchange rate was £1 = $2.40.

In July 1984 you closed the account when the exchange rate was £1 = $1.32.

A chargeable gain arises, calculated as follows:

	£
Sterling value of dollars deposited 20,000 ÷ 2.40	8,333
Sterling value of dollars when account closed 20,000 ÷ 1.32	15,151
Chargeable gain	6,818

There is, however, one exception to this rule. If the foreign currency was acquired to provide or maintain a home abroad or for other personal expenditure for you, your family or your dependents when abroad, then no charge to CGT arises on the withdrawal of money from the account.

14 Building or improving your home

14.1 If you build your own home

If you build your own home, or buy land and arrange for a builder to build a house on that land for you, you will be concerned in particular with the application of value added tax (VAT). There are also some precautions you must take to ensure that interest you pay on money you borrow for the purpose continues to be allowable for tax purposes, and you will also be concerned with the application of stamp duty (Chapter 15).

14.2 Value added tax

Although value added tax is payable in respect of money which you expend after 31 May 1984 on improving, extending or altering your home, the same will not apply if your home is built for you or if you build it yourself.

14.3 Building it yourself

If you build your own home you will have to buy all the material such as bricks, cement, timber, sanitary fittings, etc. and all of the goods which you buy will already have suffered VAT at a rate of 15%.

You may reclaim the VAT from Customs and Excise (even though you are not a person who has registered for VAT under the regulations for VAT registration) in the following circumstances:

(a) You must have purchased the materials yourself for the purpose of building the home. You must not have purchased the materials in connection with some business carried on by you.

(b) The materials must have been used on the construction of your home or on the site.

(c) You must have purchased (or imported) the goods after 13 November 1974.

(d) The materials or goods must be of the sort which themselves would have normally been incorporated into a newly built house.

14.4   What sort of items can you claim to recover the VAT for?

(a) Ordinary building materials.

(b) Builders' hardware, sanitary ware or other articles of the kind ordinarily installed by builders.

It is not always clear whether an item to be installed will be accepted by Customs and Excise as an item 'ordinarily installed by builders as fixtures'. Some things which have been accepted as ordinarily installed would be the heating system (which would include a gas fire), thermostatically controlled radiators forming part of an electrical central heating service, a cooker hood. Some things have not been accepted as ordinarily installed by builders, for example, refrigerator, sauna accessories, free-standing or wall-mounted electric fires or fitted carpets (even though they were necessary to deaden sound in a block of flats).

14.5   If you are in any doubt concerning any item which you purchase you should ask your local Customs and Excise officer.

If you intend to undertake do-it-yourself building it is a wise precaution first to obtain a copy of Customs and Excise VAT Notice No. 719.

If you do undertake do-it-yourself building but you employ a subcontractor to do specialist work, you cannot recover the VAT which may be charged to you by that subcontractor in respect of his work.

If you do carry out do-it-yourself building your claims for repayment of VAT must be made to Customs and Excise within three months of completion, although a late claim may be accepted in exceptional circumstances. You must complete a number of forms required by Customs and Excise as follows:

(a) Form VAT 431 — the claim form itself.
(b) Form VAT 432 — the description of your home and a statement of the quantities of materials used in the creation of the home.
(c) Form VAT 433 — a summary of the invoices carrying VAT (tax invoices) in respect of which you are reclaiming VAT.
(d) Form VAT 434 — a summary of invoices with less details.

You must attach a 'Certificate of Completion of Habitation' from a local authority, or alternatively some other evidence of completion or a certificate which may be required by your building society or other lender to satisfy the lender that the building is complete. You must also provide the original invoices from the suppliers in respect of which you are making the claim and, if you have directly imported any materials, then the documents showing the tax paid on import.

14.6 VAT on a home built for you

There are two ways in which a home may be built for you. The most common will be if you approach a builder who is

constructing an estate of houses or a block of flats, and contract
to purchase from the builder a completed house or flat. Usually
under such arrangements you will deal with only a single
supplier, i.e., the builder. You will have to make stage payments
during the period of construction and there will be a point of
time at which the builder will have completed his work and will
hand over the property to you as 'completed'. In such
circumstances the builder will not charge you any VAT on the
supply of your home and he will have recovered the VAT on
money which he has expended in building the home because the
construction is 'zero-rated'.

You will still suffer some VAT even if you buy a brand new
home because a solicitor or a surveyor whom you pay for his or
her services in connection with the purchase will have to charge
you VAT on top of his or her own fees, even though it is a newly
constructed home which you are buying.

If the surveyor who is engaged in connection with the purchase
of your home (whether newly constructed or not) is an employee
of a building society, then the survey fee is treated as part of the
cost of the borrowing for VAT purposes and is 'exempt' from
VAT. If, however, the building society employs an independent
surveyor to survey the property on its behalf, or you engage a
surveyor to survey the property on your behalf, VAT will be
payable on that surveyor's fees.

14.7   What are the rules for VAT if you engage a builder to construct a home for you?

If you buy land and engage an architect, for example, to design a
home for you which is then built for you either by a single
builder or perhaps by a number of contractors, then the
individual contractors will be entitled not to charge you VAT in
respect of their invoices to you provided you are constructing a
new home (i.e., the work is zero-rated). If there was a house

standing on the site before then the cost of demolishing the previous structure would also be zero-rated.

14.8 In these circumstances you would still have to suffer VAT in respect of:

(a) The services of an architect.
(b) The services of a surveyor or any other person acting as a consultant or supervisor.
(c) The services supplied to you not in the course of the business of the person supplying it.
(d) Services which represent an undivided share in property or the possession of goods.
(e) Services which represent a charge for the use of goods not for business purposes.

14.9 Value added tax and improvements or alterations

The rules in respect of VAT and improvements or alterations to property changed with effect from 1 June 1984. Prior to that date, goods or services supplied in connection with the improvement or alteration of an existing property were zero-rated so that the supplier would not have to charge VAT in respect of them. Any goods or services supplied after 31 May 1984 will suffer VAT at the rate of 15%. The key to establishing whether VAT is payable is whether the 'tax point' in respect of the supply of the goods or services is before or after 1 June 1984.

The tax point in respect of the supply of goods or services is usually the earliest of:

(a) For a supply of goods, the date the goods were actually supplied.
(b) For a supply of services, the date the services were actually supplied.

(c) The date you actually pay, even if this is before any goods or services have been invoiced or supplied.
(d) The date the goods or services are invoiced to you.*

If you paid the builder or other supplier before 1 June 1984 then the date of payment is the tax point. The date of the contract and *in this particular case* the date on which invoices are rendered will be ignored.

14.10 In respect of money spent on alterations or improvements to 'listed' buildings money spent on alterations or improvements after 31 May 1984, may still be zero-rated.

14.11 Money borrowed to finance improvements
(FA 1972, sch. 9, para. 1(6))

If you already own your own home, and borrow money to extend or improve it, then the interest paid on the amount borrowed will be treated as allowable interest provided the total of your original borrowing to acquire the home and the money you borrow for improvements does not exceed £30,000. If the total borrowed does exceed £30,000, then only a proportion of the new borrowing which brings your total borrowing up to £30,000 will rank for relief.

14.11.1 Example 14A You purchased your home in 1981 for £40,000 and borrowed what was then the maximum amount which ranked for relief, i.e., £25,000. In 1983 you extended your home giving you two new bedrooms and a new bathroom, together with an extended kitchen. The cost of the extension was £12,000 and you borrowed £10,000 in order to finance the extension.

The interest which you pay in 1984/85 on the original £25,000 loan is £2,750.

The interest which you pay in 1984/85 in respect of the £10,000 you borrowed for your improvements is £1,200. The amount of mortgage interest will be calculated as follows:

	£
Original borrowing	25,000
Interest payable	2,750

Further borrowing of £10,000. Interest payable £1,200
Allowable: $\dfrac{(30,000 - 25,000)}{10,000} \times £1,200$ 600

Total allowable interest   3,350

14.12 What items of expenditure are treated as 'improvements'? *(IR11, Appendix)*

The following items would be accepted as improvements so that money borrowed to finance them would rank for interest relief.

(a) Home extensions and loft conversions.
(b) Central heating installation (but not portable radiators or night storage heaters).
(c) The installation of double-glazing including detachable double-glazing.
(d) Insulation of a roof or walls.
(e) Installation of bathrooms or other plumbing.
(f) Kitchen units, such as sinks or fitted kitchen units which are to and become part of the building.
(g) Connections to main drainage.
(h) Construction of garage or garden shed or a greenhouse.
(i) The construction or landscaping of gardens.
(j) The construction of a swimming-pool.
(k) The division of a property into two flats or the building on of a granny flat.
(l) The concreting or improvement of driveways or paths.
(m) The installation of new electrical wiring (but not the replacement of previous wiring).

14.13   *(FA 1972, sch. 9, para. 3)*

A number of items of expenditure are not treated as
'improvements'. These would be items of repairs and
maintenance which do not improve the property but make it
good, prevent deterioration or make good the ravages of time,
wind and weather. If you purchase a property in a dilapidated
state, however, then the initial cost to repair and put it in order is
treated as part of the original purchase price (and not an
improvement although the money borrowed will be treated as
part of the money borrowed for the original purchase).

The Inland Revenue will allow you to include in the cost of
improvement any consequential redecoration or repair incurred
in carrying out an improvement. This would apply particularly
to improvements for which you may have got a grant under the
provisions of the Housing Acts 1969 to 1974.

14.14   Improvements and CGT   *(CGTA, s. 32; sch. 5
para. 11; FA 1982, s. 86)*

If you expend money for the improvement of your home, and
the improvement is reflected in the value of the property when
you sell it, then the money you spend on the improvement will
be added to the original cost of the property when computing
any capital gains tax which you may have to pay (see 8.18).

These items of expenditure on improvement will be increased
by the indexation allowance applicable to increases in the Retail
Prices Index 12 months after the date that the improvement is
made (see 8.36).

If your property was purchased before 6 April 1965 (see 8.25)
then the gain attributable to the improvement must be
separately analysed and apportioned.

The apportionment is made by adding all the expenditure

incurred on acquiring or improving the property (see 8.18), and deducting the total from the proceeds of sale. The *gain* calculated in this way is then divided between the various items of expenditure in the ratio they bear individually to the total expenditure incurred.

The part of the gain attributable to each item of expenditure is then *individually* divided as explained in paragraph 8.25, and that part treated as having arisen after 6 April 1965 is chargeable to CGT. This can be particularly disadvantageous if substantial expenditure has been incurred after 5 April 1965.

14.15 Improvements to a home acquired before 6 April 1965 *(CGTA, sch. 5, para. 11(5))*

There is one very useful exception to the rule that a proportion of the total gain must be attributable to the expenditure which gave rise to it.

If you acquired your home for a cost which is very small in relation to the value of your home when you spend money to improve it then the money spent on improvement will be treated much as if it had been expended at the date you originally acquired the property. This rule will only apply if you originally acquired your home before 6 April 1965.

14.15.1 Example 14B You inherited your home in 1950 on the death of your father and the house was then valued at £1,200.

In 1980 you found the home was too small for you and expended £6,000 constructing a garage with a bedroom and bathroom over it. In 1980 immediately before you carried out the extension the house was worth £38,000. Because the 'cost' of the house when you acquired it in 1950 was only £1,200 (this was small having regard to the value of the asset immediately before you extended the property), you may treat the cost of the extension much as if it had been expended in 1950 when you inherited the property, and as if you had expended in 1950 the money which you in fact paid out in 1980, so that your *original* cost is increased to £7,200.

15 Stamp duty

15.1 *(SA 1891, s. 54)*

Stamp duty is one of the oldest taxes applicable in Great Britain. It is payable in respect of documents by which any property or interest or estate in property is conveyed or transferred.

15.2 In the case of a small number of transactions the rate of duty will be only 50p. This is a 'fixed duty'. The majority however are liable to a rate of 1% of the value concerned.

If a document which is supposed to transfer a property is not properly stamped two consequences will follow:

(a) The document would be inadmissible as evidence in court. For example, you could not say that you had purchased your home if the document were not properly stamped.

(b) If and when the document is subject to stamping there may be penalties payable.

15.3 Stamp duty in respect of a sale of land (which would include a house on it)

If you buy a home, then if the cost of your home exceeds £30,000 you will have to pay tax at 1% of the cost. If you buy your home under an arrangement where you buy from the vendor, not only the structure and the things fixed to the structure, but also some of the contents of his home, such as, for example, a cooker or refrigerator, carpets, curtains or light fittings, then the price which you pay for the contents will not be included in the total which is chargeable for stamp duty. The price attributable to the contents must be reasonable having regard to the alternative cost to you of acquiring those items.

15.4   If you are having a house built for you (see 14.7) then the stamp duty will be payable only on the cost of the land and not on the cost of the construction. This rule may not apply if you purchase the land from the person who ultimately does the building for you.

15.5   *(PR 1957)*

If you do buy land from somebody who also does the building for you the rules for determining on what you pay stamp duty are as follows:

(a)   If your contracts are simultaneous for the purchase of the land and for the building work then stamp duty is payable on the land only, provided that:

  (i)   the building work has not already commenced; and
  (ii) your entitlement to acquire the land is not dependent upon the building work.

(b)   If you are only entitled to have the land conveyed to you when the building is finished you must pay stamp duty on the whole cost of the building and the land.

(c)   If you purchase a building which is partly constructed at the time of purchase, then if you are entitled to have the land conveyed to you at the time you purchase it, stamp duty will be payable on the price of the land plus so much of the price as is attributable to the building work which was completed before the land is conveyed to you.

(d)   If the contract and price of constructing the building does not include consideration for the land, i.e., you have engaged a builder separately, then stamp duty will be payable only on the consideration for the land.

15.6 What stamp duty is payable if you exchange your home for another? *(SA 1891, s. 73)*

If you exchange your home for a home belonging to some other person, for example, you move from Nottingham to Bristol and buy a home from somebody who moves from Bristol to Nottingham and each of you moves into the other's home, then if no money passes hands stamp duty is payable at only 50p on the transaction. If, as is likely, some money does pass hands then stamp duty will be payable at 1% on the amount which is paid to equalise the value.

15.7 On what is stamp duty payable?

If you purchase your home and pay outright for it then the price which you pay is based upon the consideration and not on any underlying value of the land and buildings which you acquire.

15.8 What happens if you arrange to pay by instalments?

If you arrange to pay your purchase price by instalments then stamp duty will be payable at the time you purchase the property on the total of all the instalments. No discount will be allowed for the deferment. If you pay interest on instalments then the interest portion of the instalments which you pay will be excluded from the stamp duty computation.

15.9 *(FA 1981, s. 107)*

If you purchase your home from a local council or buy property in circumstances where you may have to make an additional payment to the vendor (if, for example, you sell the property within a short time after buying it) then such additional payments or discount are ignored for the purpose of calculating stamp duty. The stamp duty is payable on the amount that you pay at the time you buy the property.

15.10   *(SA 1891, s. 57)*

If you buy a property which is subject to a mortgage so that you agree to take over responsibility for the existing mortgage or for some other liability then you must pay stamp duty on the total price plus the liabilities you have assumed. If you acquire your home in satisfaction of money which somebody borrowed from you then you will pay stamp duty on the amount of the debt which is satisfied or, if the debt is satisfied by a property whose value is less than the debt, by the value of the property at the date you acquire it.

15.11   When is the stamp duty payable and by whom?   *(SA 1891, s. 58)*

Stamp duty is payable when the property which you buy is conveyed. If you sign a contract to buy a home and then decide not to proceed with the purchase, and then find a purchaser who will take over your contract, the liability for stamp duty falls not on you but on the person who takes over the contract from you.

If you buy a property then your solicitor who arranges the conveyance must certify the value attributable to stamp duty in respect of that and any connected transactions. This rule prevents you dividing a transaction up into slices of less than £30,000 on each of which no stamp duty would be payable.

15.12   Stamp duty and leases

There is stamp duty in respect of certain transactions other than the purchase of properties, in particular in regard to leases. If the term of the lease is less than seven years and the rent is more than £500 a year then stamp duty would be payable at the rate of

50p per £50 or part of £50 of the rent. If the term of the lease is between seven and 35 years stamp duty would be payable at £1 per £50 or part of £50 of the rent. If the term is over 35 but under 100 years stamp duty would be £6 per £50 rent or part of £50. If the term exceeds 100 years stamp duty would be at a rate of £12 per £50 or part of £50. This scale of stamp duty would apply only if the rent exceeds £500 per annum. There are special provisions for charging stamp duty (a) on a premium payable on the grant of a lease and (b) on furnished lettings.

There are provisions which counteract artificial arrangements which attempt to treat sales of property as if they are only leases.

16   Tax and working at home

If you use your home as a place from which part of your work is done, then this may have a bearing on your income tax, on the capital gains tax that you might have to pay if you sold your home and on the capital transfer tax (see 9.14) which might be payable on a gift of your home or on your death.

16.1   Travel to and from your home

16.1.1   *If you are an employee*   *(ICTA, s. 189(1))*   If you are employed by somebody else whose place of business is some distance from your own home, then the Inland Revenue will not allow you to claim as a deductible expense the cost of travel from your home to your employer's place of business. In order for such travel expenses to be allowable, you would have to show that they were wholly, exclusively and necessarily expended in the conduct of your employment. The problem lies in the term 'necessarily'. It is established that the word 'necessarily' means necessary for any person who had your job and not the individual who happens to have it, i.e., you. The argument is that it is you who choose to live the way you do and some other persons who had your job might live somewhere different and have different or no travelling costs.

16.1.2   It may be that your employer requires you to work at a number of different locations. You may rarely visit your employer's place of business if, for example, you are employed by a manufacturer to service washing-machines. In practice, you may travel directly to a number of different places each day starting from home. In such a case your travel expenses from

home will be an allowable expense (if not reimbursed to you by your employer) although, strictly speaking, you would only be allowed to claim the difference in cost between travelling from home to your employer's place of business and the actual places you do visit. The Inland Revenue do not usually enforce this strict rule.

16.1.3 If your employer asks you to travel to some location other than the one at which you normally work (he asks you to work in his Glasgow office whereas you normally work in his Bristol office) then the cost of travelling from home to the employer's other location will be an allowable expense.

16.1.4 *(FA 1977, s. 32)* If you take a job with an overseas employer and your work is carried out wholly abroad, then the cost of travelling from your home to your new employment at the beginning of the employment and the costs of returning at the end of the employment are regarded as having been necessarily incurred in the performance of your duties, and so may be claimed as an allowable expense. (There are certain restrictions which may apply if you are not domiciled (see 13.2) within the UK and your employer is not resident in the UK.)

16.2 If you are self-employed or work for your own company *(ICTA, s. 130)*

The very restrictive conditions under which travel may be an allowable expense for somebody who is employed are relaxed in the case of somebody who works for himself. In practice, some of these relaxations may also apply to a 'one-man company'. If you are self-employed and your home is the base of your self-employment, then any travelling expenses incurred wholly and exclusively in connection with your work will be an allowable expense. It is important to notice that if the purpose of your journey is mixed then, strictly speaking, none of its costs will be allowable for tax although by concession your Inspector of Taxes may allow you to apportion some of the costs. If, for example, you are a doctor and you practise from home, then if you travel to a medical conference in Spain but stay a few days longer than the period of the conference, the Inspector of Taxes will argue that your travel was for a dual purpose. In that case he will seek to disallow either the whole or part of your travel costs and certainly the whole of your costs in Spain other than during the conference.

If you are, for example, a solicitor working in practice in the town centre, you may well take work home. Although there may be some consequences in connection with your home itself (see 16.9), you will not be able to argue that because you took work home each night, the cost of travelling to work and back home again, carrying the work you did at home, would be an allowable expense for tax purposes. You would have travelled from work to home in any event so that there were no costs incurred 'wholly and exclusively' in the conduct of your profession.

16.3   One-man companies

Many individuals who work for themselves are not 'self-employed' but have a limited company of which they are a director. You may, for example, be a tree surgeon and own a company, XYZ Ltd. You are perhaps the only director and you and your wife are the only shareholders. In practice, all your travelling expenses from home will be allowable. XYZ Ltd may have its registered office (its legal address) at your own home or elsewhere, for example, at your accountants' office. If the registered office is at your own home, then by definition that is *the* place of business of the company so that although you are an employee (all the directors are employees of the company for which they work) you will be working from the place of business of the company. The same would be true even if the registered office were at your accountants' office but there was a 'place of business' of the company at your own home. If there is a place of business at your own home, then any travel from there to wherever the registered office might be kept would be for travel for the purpose of the company's business. If you conduct your business from home this may affect your rates (see 17.10).

16.4 Working from home: the costs of your home

Whether you are employed or self-employed, you may incur costs in working at home. If you are employed then such costs could only be claimed if your employer required you to work from home. If he does not require you to work from home under the terms of your contract of employment, then you cannot argue that it is 'necessary' for the purpose of your employment that you do the work at home. You may say that you feel it is necessary, but it is not a requirement of your employment. If you wish to argue with your Inspector of Taxes that you do have to work from home, you should obtain confirmation from your employer that he *requires* you to do some part of your work at home. Perhaps you have to write a report on what you have done during the day — many sales representatives have to do this. Such a confirmation will not cost your employer anything, and it may be worthwhile talking to your employer if you do not already have such a provision in your terms of employment. You can then claim the extra costs of working at home or a proportion of your total costs as explained below as being deductible from your earnings (but not travel from home to your place of employment).

16.5 What expenses can you claim as allowable for income tax?

If you use a portion of your home for your work, then any of the expenses which are set out in 7.1 might be allowable expenses. In practice, however, there are some costs which are more commonly claimed in the case of people who work from home and these are:

(a) Additional costs of heating (you might work late and keep your central heating on later than usual).

(b) Additional costs of cleaning.

(c) The costs of calls on your telephone (but not the cost of rental).

(d) Additional lighting costs.

(e) If, for example, you are a doctor and have a surgery at home, additional costs of cleaning or decoration caused by people coming to you at home.

16.6   *(CGTA, s. 103)*

The rules for capital gains tax in connection with exemptions on the sale of your home apply only to the extent that your home is occupied exclusively as a home, so you should not claim that a room or rooms are used *exclusively* for the purpose of your work (see 16.9). Such exclusive use may also affect the rates which you pay (see 17.10).

If you rent your home, you may argue that a proportion of the rent which you pay is an allowable expense for income tax purposes. If you rent a four-roomed flat and one room is used wholly for the purpose of your work, then there is no good reason why a quarter of the rent should not be claimed as an allowable expense. A similar claim to tax relief in respect of rates would apply whether you own or rent your home. You cannot, however, argue that the mortgage repayments were an allowable expense.

16.6.1 *Example 16A* You work as a freelance designer in one room in a four-roomed flat which you rent furnished for £2,000 p.a. Your annual outgoings are as follows:

	£
Rent	2,000
Rates	180
Heating and lighting	300
Insurance	60
	2,540

You can claim £2,540 × ¼ = £635 as accommodation costs when submitting the return of your income to your Inspector of Taxes.

16.7 Buying your home and working from it

If you wish to buy a property with a view both to living in it and working from it, then you may be able to claim that interest paid on a mortgage of more than £30,000 will be deductible for income tax purposes. Basically, you will be allowed to claim as an allowable expense for tax purposes interest which you pay on money borrowed for the purpose of your occupation or profession (but not if you are an employee). An example of this sort of circumstance would be if you were a doctor or dentist who purchased a large house a proportion of which was used in the conduct of your medical or dental practice. Another circumstance would be if you purchased a shop with a flat over it.

16.7.1 Example 16B You are a chiropodist and you wish to buy a house at a cost of £60,000. You estimate you will have to spend a further £5,000 adapting two of the rooms from which to conduct your profession as a chiropodist. The house has six rooms (other than bathroom, kitchen, etc.). You have £20,000 yourself from the sale of your previous home from which you did not conduct your profession. You pay interest at 10% i.e. £4,500 a year on your total borrowing of £45,000 necessary to buy and adapt the house. The amount of *mortgage interest* relief which you may claim is still limited to the interest which you pay on £30,000, i.e., £3,000.

When you prepare your accounts as a self-employed chiropodist, however, in addition to the costs of running your home attributable to the chiropody practice, you may claim as an ordinary business expense the appropriate proportion of the total interest which you pay. If this is the case the proportion would be the number of rooms used for your profession (two) divided by total number of rooms in the house (six), i.e., one-third, so that the relief which you claim in your business computations would be £4,500 × ⅓ = £1,500.

16.7.2   *Example 16C*   If instead of six rooms, the house had had only five rooms, the total interest which you could claim would still not exceed the total interest which you paid. What you calculate would be the interest attributable to your profession, i.e., total interest paid (£4,500) × number of rooms used in your profession (two) ÷ the number of rooms in the house (five) = £1,800, and you would then claim the remaining interest payable but not exceeding the interest payable on £30,000 as an allowable expense in your general tax computations.

16.7.3   *Example 16D*   Using the same figures again, assume you have bought a house with seven rooms of which two were used for your profession for the same cost and with the same financing costs. Your allowable mortgage interest relief would be limited to the interest on £30,000, i.e., it would still be £3,000. To calculate the interest allowable in your professional accounts, you would be able to claim as an ordinary business cost, £4,500 × number of rooms used in your profession (two) divided by number of rooms in the house (seven), so that your allowable interest would then be £1,286. You will notice in this case that a proportion of the total interest you pay, £4,500 minus (£3,000 plus £1,286), i.e., £214, would *not* have been allowed in any way for income tax.

You might, however, argue that of the total money which you borrowed, only £40,000 was expended to acquire the property and £5,000 was expended specifically to adapt the property for the purposes of your profession.

If you claim that of your total borrowings, £5,000 related wholly to your profession, so that £40,000 was used to purchase the property, your allowable mortgage interest relief would be calculated as follows:

£

Money borrowed for the purpose of your profession:
Adaptation costs   5,000

Proportion of total borrowings relating to business:

$$\frac{\text{number of rooms used for profession (2)}}{\text{total number of rooms (7)}} \times £40,000 = 11,429$$

Total money borrowed for purpose of profession   16,429

Interest thereon @ 10%   1,643

Total borrowed to purchase your home   45,000
Less: Attributable to business   16,429

Balance = money borrowed to purchase your home   28,571

The total borrowings used to purchase your home are now less than £30,000 so that the whole of the interest would be an allowable expense, £1,643 being claimed as a business expense, and £2,857 as mortgage interest relief.

16.7.4 Example 16E   You wish to buy a music shop with a flat over it, in which you intend to live and which you intend to make your home. The building, including all the shop fittings (but not including stock) costs £60,000. You have £20,000 of your own savings which you apply to the purchase, and borrow £40,000 on a loan account from your bank. How can you calculate what proportion of your total borrowings relates to your home, and what proportion to the business you have purchased? There is no hard and fast rule to determine this. If the residential part of the property is separately rated (see 17.10) then the Inspector of Taxes may suggest that the proportion of rateable value of the whole which is attributable to the residential part is the proportion of the borrowing which you have applied in the acquisition of your home:

$$\frac{\text{proportion of rateable value (300)}}{\text{total rateable value (300 + 500)}} \times \text{total borrowings} (\pounds40,000)$$

= £15,000

Interest payable on £15,000 will be claimed as mortgage interest relief. The balance of the borrowings (£25,000) will be attributed to the acquisition of the business and the interest on the £25,000 will be claimed as an ordinary business expense.

Frequently, however, the residential accommodation will not be separately rated. In that case you will have to negotiate with the Inspector of Taxes how the interest which you pay should be apportioned. Strictly speaking, the loan has to be apportioned 'in proportion to the expenditure on business and residential purposes'. Since there is no ready way to find out what that proportion is, you will find that the Inspector of Taxes will accept any reasonable method of arriving at that proportion.

16.8   *(ICTA, s. 175)*

If you have a choice in respect of interest which you pay, either to claim that it is interest on your 'principal private residence' or that it is interest paid for the purposes of your business, you may choose which of the two bases you wish to apply. Once you have chosen which basis you will apply in respect of a particular loan, you cannot change your mind afterwards. If, however, you have chosen to claim relief as 'mortgage interest relief' for your principal private residence, but your total income for the year is not sufficient to absorb that relief, then the unrelieved amount of the interest may be carried forward (or if the business has ceased, backwards) as if it were a business loss.

16.9   Working from home: capital gains tax

As explained in Chapter 8 if you occupy a property as your sole or main residence, then you will not be chargeable for capital gains tax in respect of a gain made on the disposal of that property. This rule is limited if you do not occupy the property 'exclusively' as your sole or main residence. If you work from home but do not use any part of your home *exclusively* for the purposes of your work, then the fact that you work at home will have no bearing on the capital gains tax treatment of the future sale of the property. If you do use one or more rooms exclusively for the purposes of your profession or occupation, then that part of your home will not enjoy the exemption from capital gains tax usually available for your main residence. (See also 11.12 for DLT consequences, and 17.10 for effect on rates.)

16.10 Income tax and capital gains tax: working from home

You will notice that, as explained in 16.4 and 16.5, you may be able to claim certain expenses for income tax purposes as allowable if you work from home. It is *not* necessarily the case that such a claim will automatically mean that the part of your home in which you work has now ceased to be your sole or main residence for capital gains tax purposes. For example, if you are a self-employed journalist and you work from home, you may well use one of your rooms as a study in which you do your work. You keep your books and reference information in your study and your typewriter and desk there. If, however, you also keep a convertible bed in the room so that when guests come to stay in the house they can stay in your study, then your room is not used 'exclusively' for that purpose of your profession. Even if you argue for income tax purposes that the proportion of the expenses of your home relating to your occupation of that room is an allowable expense, the facts of the matter are that the room is not used 'exclusively' for the purpose of your profession. The same would be true if, for example, there was a television in the room which your family watched from time to time (but not while you were working there!).

It is very important, if you do claim for income tax purposes that you use the room for the purpose of your work, that you make clear when you first make your claim for income tax purposes that the room concerned, although used substantially, is not used *exclusively* for the purpose of your work.

16.11 How is the calculation of capital gains tax affected by working from home?

If you do use a room or rooms exclusively for the purposes of your work then the proportion of your home represented by those rooms will, if sold, be chargeable to capital gains tax on sale.

16.11.1 Example 16F In example 16B you purchased a home with six rooms for a total cost (including adaptation to your chiropodist practice) of £65,000 on 30 June 1980. On 30 June 1985 you sell the property at £92,000. Your selling costs are £2,500. The computation of the amount of the proceeds of sale chargeable to capital gains tax is as set out below:

	£	£
Sale proceeds June 1985		92,000
Less:		
Cost of property	65,000	
Indexation relief (see 8.37 to 8.40)	6,500	
Cost of sale	2,500	
		74,000
Gain		18,000

Exempt:

$$\frac{\text{number of rooms used as main residence (4)}}{\text{number of rooms in house (6)}} \times £18,000 \quad 12,000$$

Chargeable to CGT		6,000

16.12 Re-investing your sale proceeds: rollover relief *(CGTA, s. 115)*

You may be able to defer any charge to capital gains tax on the sale of your home, part of which was used for your work, if you re-invest the proceeds of sale.

The rules are that first you must calculate what fraction of your home was used for business purposes.

Then you must apply that fraction to the proceeds of sale (and not to the gain) which you receive on selling your home.

If you expend an amount at least equal to the resultant figure, within a period commencing 12 months before the date of sale (see 8.17) and ending three years after the date of sale, in purchasing appropriate assets (see 16.13) used in connection with that or any other trade or profession which you carry on, then you can defer any charge to capital gains tax as explained below.

16.13 What, for the purposes of rollover relief, are appropriate assets? *(CGTA, s. 118)*

In order to be able to claim rollover relief the new assets which you buy must fit into one of a number of categories. These are:

(a) Any building or part of a building occupied and used only for the purposes of the trade or profession.
(b) Any land occupied and used only for the purpose of the trade or profession.
(c) Fixed plant or machinery which has not formed part of a building.
(d) Ships, aircraft and hovercraft.
(e) Goodwill.
(f) Woodlands where the woodlands are managed on a

commercial basis and with a view to the realisation of profits.

(g)   Furnished holiday accommodation (see 7.16).

16.14   In the context of your home, what you may well do, having sold a home part of which was used for the purposes of your work, would be to buy another home part of which was used for the same purpose. Provided the appropriate fraction of your new home costs at least as much as the fraction of the sale proceeds of your other home, then instead of paying capital gains tax on the sale of your first home, you may reduce the cost of the new home by the amount which would otherwise have been chargeable to capital gains tax and treat the cost of the new home as reduced accordingly.

16.14.1   Example 16G   In example 16F the sale proceeds of your home as a chiropodist were £92,000 less cost of sale £2,500, i.e. £89,500. What fraction of this was attributable to your trade or profession?

$$\frac{\text{number of rooms used for profession (2)}}{\text{total number of rooms (6)}} \times £89,500 = £29,833$$

You must spend at least £29,833 in respect of the part of your new home which you use for your chiropody practice in order to defer the charge to CGT on the gain of £6,000 you made on the sale.

Suppose your new home costs £100,000 and it has eight rooms, two of which you intend to use for the purposes of your chiropody practice. You spend £5,000 to adapt those two rooms for the purposes of your chiropody practice.

Calculate the fraction of your new home used for the purpose of your trade or profession:

£

$$\frac{\text{number of rooms used for profession (2)}}{\text{total number of rooms (8)}}$$

× cost of new home (£100,000)	=	25,000

Add: Cost of adaptation	5,000
Total expended on proportion of new home used in chiropody practice	30,000

This exceeds the fraction of your sale proceeds attributable to the sale of your previous home, i.e. £29,833, so you do not have to pay CGT on the sale of your old home.

The cost of your new home, for capital gains tax purposes, will be adjusted as follows:

	£
Purchase cost of property	100,000
Add: Cost of adaptation	5,000
	105,000
Less: Chargeable gain on sale of previous house rolled over	6,000
Adjusted cost of new home carried forward	99,000

It might be that the new home which you have purchased was already adapted as a chiropodist's practice and that the chiropodist from whom you bought it said that in addition to £100,000 for his home, he wanted £5,000 for the goodwill of his existing practice. In that case you may add the cost of the goodwill (i.e., £5,000) to the fraction of the cost of the home used for the purpose of your profession (i.e., the £25,000 referred to above), giving a total expended for the purposes of your profession on appropriate assets of £30,000.

16.15   What happens if you do not re-invest the whole proceeds of sale?   *(CGTA, s. 116)*

If the amount which you re-invest in appropriate assets is less than the fraction attributable to business occupation of the proceeds of sale of your home when you sold it, you may still make a partial claim to rollover relief provided that the amount you re-invest is at least equal to the *cost* of the assets which were sold. The gain which is chargeable is then equal to the amount which is not invested.

When rollover relief is to be claimed, it is not necessary that the money expended on the new assets comes from the proceeds of sale of the old assets.

This would mean, for example, that if the new assets were purchased with money borrowed for the purpose, the interest would be allowable for tax purposes even though the same expenditure gave you a deferral for capital gains tax purpose. It would even be possible that a proportion of the money which you expend would rank for capital allowances (see Glossary) even though the expenditure of that money allowed you to claim rollover relief.

16.16   Capital transfer tax

As explained in 9.14, where a proportion of your home is used for business purposes, the value to be taken into account in calculating capital transfer tax may be abated.

16.17   Working for yourself in a home provided by somebody else   *(FA 1984, s. 25)*

As explained in 2.17, if you are an employee and work in job-related accommodation you are entitled to certain reliefs. It may be, however, that you are self-employed but the home in which you work is closely allied to your self-employment. An example would be if you were a self-employed publican working in brewery tied accommodation.

In order to qualify within these provisions, it is necessary that:

(a) You (or your spouse) must be carrying on a trade, profession or vocation from your home.
(b) The home must be provided by some other person.
(c) You must be bound by contract to carry out your work but live in those premises.

You may not enjoy the relief if you are connected in some way with the person who owns the property. You (or your spouse) must not have a material interest in the company providing the accommodation nor may you (or your spouse) be in partnership with any such person. If you are self-employed but your home falls within the definition of job-related accommodation, then you may claim interest relief in respect of another home which you purchased as if you were employed (see 2.17) and for capital gains tax purposes (see 8.46) claim the same relief as if you were in job-related accommodation as an employee.

16.18 Capital gains tax: retirement relief *(CGTA, s. 124; FA 1984, s. 63)*

There is a further possible exemption which you may enjoy if you have occupied a part of your home in connection with your business or trade. If you are aged over 60 when you sell your home, and you have occupied your home partly for the purpose of your trade or profession for at least 12 months before the date of sale, any gain which would otherwise be chargeable to capital gains tax may be exempt from CGT to some extent. The maximum exemption which you can claim is £100,000 and this will be reduced by two fractions:

(a) Number of years you have used your home for the
      purposes of your trade (up to a maximum of 10) ÷ 10.
(b) Number of months by which you are older than 60 (not
      exceeding 60 months) ÷ 60.

16.18.1 *Example 16H* You are aged 63 and you are a doctor
who has conducted a surgery from your home for the last five
years.

The gain on the sale of your home which would be chargeable to
capital gains tax if you do not claim retirement relief is £50,000.

16.19 How much 'retirement relief' can you claim?

The maximum amount of retirement relief which you can claim
is £100,000 × the years you have conducted the trade (5) over
maximum period (10) × number of months you are over age 60
(36) ÷ maximum number of months (60). This arithmetical
calculation gives an exempt amount of £30,000.

You may deduct £30,000 from the gain attributable to the
business use of your home, so leaving only £20,000 as
chargeable to CGT.

16.20 Income tax relief on your farmhouse *(ESC B.5, s. 79; s. 170)*

If you live on a farm which the Inland Revenue do not accept is
run commercially (often called 'hobby farming') then after five
years of losses, you may not claim such losses as trading losses
for income tax purposes.

In such circumstances you may claim the money which you
spend on maintenance, repairs and insurance of the land and
buildings which constitute the farm, as if the expense were a

capital allowance — you may include *one-third* of such expenditure on your home if it is the farmhouse.

The claim is firstly against income from agricultural land, but if you have insufficient or no income from agricultural land, you may claim to set off such expenditure against your general income.

17   *Rates*

Apart from the taxes charged by central government, such as income tax, capital gains tax, capital transfer tax and value added tax, the tax which is most commonly met by individuals is 'rates'. Rates are charged by local authorities, whether they be a parish council, a borough, a county council or a metropolitan council, and they are charged on the occupation of land. If you occupy land, then you are likely to be charged with rates.

17.1   Who is an occupier?

There are certain cases where, even if you occupy a house, you will not be the person who is charged with rates.

The most common example would be if you are an employee and live in premises provided by your employer and:

(a)   It is essential for the performance of your duties that you occupy the particular house you do or live within a closely defined perimeter; or

(b)   Although it is not essential for you to occupy a particular house or live within a particular perimeter, you can better perform your duties as an employee to a material degree *and* there is an express term in your contract of employment that you shall reside in such a home.

If the occupation of your home falls within these particular definitions then it is your employer and not you who is 'the occupier' and therefore is liable to pay rates in respect of your occupation of your home.

17.2 If, on the other hand, you provide a home for an employee, because it is convenient for you to do so, or perhaps because there is no other housing as convenient as that particular home, then your employee and not you will be liable to pay rates in respect of his home.

17.3 *(GRA 1967, s. 24)*

There is another circumstance in which the owner, rather than any particular person who lives there, may be liable to pay rates in respect of a house and that is where it has been divided for multi-occupation, not into self-contained flats. In such cases the Valuation Officer may, at his discretion, assess the whole house as if it were in single occupation and in that case it is the owner who will be liable to pay rates.

This situation can arise only if the property was originally built as a single dwelling, either wholly or in part, and is now occupied 'in parts'.

For the purposes of collection of rates for a multi-occupied dwelling-house, the 'owner' is defined as the person who receives the rents rather than the person who is entitled to receive them. This would include, for example, an agent.

It is important to notice that it is not the ownership of a home (apart from the circumstances explained above) which gives rise to a charge to rates, but the occupation of the home.

17.4 When do you 'occupy' your home?

Since any charge to rates which may fall on you as the occupier of your home can only commence from the moment in time when you are in 'occupation' it is important to know from when you are in occupation. The moment of time when you are treated as being in occupation will usually be the time when you first move furniture into your home, whether or not you yourself live there at that time. Similarly, you will cease to be liable to pay rates on your home if you remove all furniture from it.

17.5   Unoccupied rates *(GRA 1967, s. 17; sch. 1)*

There is provision, however, that local authorities may introduce regulations which charge either full or partial rates on properties which have been unoccupied for a period of not less than three months. This rate is known as unoccupied rate or, sometimes, a void rate or empty rate. The proportion of rates which may be charged in these circumstances varies from one local authority to another.

In the case of newly erected or converted dwelling-houses, the minimum period of three months is extended to six months. This is known as 'the new house period'.

Since such a property is clearly not 'occupied' the person on whom the rate will be levied will be the 'owner'.

17.6   *(GRA 1967, sch. 1)*

There are certain circumstances under which the owner of an unoccupied building will not be liable to pay the unoccupied rate. The more common of these circumstances are as follows:

(a)   Where the owner is prohibited by law from occupying the property.
(b)   Where the property is kept vacant by reason of an action taken by or on behalf of the Crown or any local or public authority with a view to prohibiting the occupation (perhaps the building has been condemned by the public health authority).
(c)   In certain circumstances if the property is a listed building

(but not all grade 3 listed buildings are included in this exemption).

(d) Where the property is available for occupation by a minister of religion as a residence from which to perform the duties of his office.

(e) If the owner is entitled to possession only in his capacity as personal representative of a deceased person.

(f) Where the owner's estate is subject to a receiving order under the Bankruptcy Act 1914.

17.7 What is rateable value? *(GRA 1967, s. 19)*

Rates are charged on the 'net annual value' of a property. The net annual value is a figure which is calculated by reference to the 'gross value' of the property. The gross value is defined as the rent at which the property might reasonably be expected to be let from year to year if the tenant undertook to pay all the usual tenant's rates and taxes and the landlord undertook to bear the costs of repairs and insurance and the other expenses, if any, necessary to maintain the property in a state to command that rent.

From the gross value is deducted an amount known as the 'statutory deduction' which is calculated as follows:

Gross value	Statutory deduction
Not exceeding £65	45% of gross value
Exceeding £65 but not exceeding £128	£29 + 30% of the amount by which the gross value exceeds £65
Exceeding £128 but not exceeding £330	£48 + 16⅔% of the amount by which the gross value exceeds £128 subject to a maximum of £80

Exceeding £330 but not exceeding £430	£80 + 20% of the amount by which the gross value exceeds £330
Exceeding £430	£100 + 16⅔% of the amount by which the gross value exceeds £430

The amount which is left by deducting the statutory deductions from the gross value is called the 'net annual value'. The net annual value is more commonly called the 'rateable value'.

17.8   You will notice that the rateable value is calculated as if your home was let. The calculation is a hypothetical one particularly because the calculation is made not based upon the rent which your home might fetch today, but on the rent which it would have fetched when the last 'valuation list' was established, which was in 1973. It will be seen that the calculation of rateable value is based upon a number of hypotheses. The calculation of rateable value becomes even more difficult where a new home is built. In order to be able to calculate the rateable value the Valuation Officer must suppose that the house (perhaps built in 1984) would have been available for letting in 1973.

Nowadays more than half the homes in Great Britain are owner-occupied, and another approximately 35% are owned by local authorities and therefore not let in the open market. The basis upon which homes are therefore rated is far away from being based on a direct comparison with market rents.

17.9   How much rates do you have to pay?   *(GRA 1967, s. 2)*

The local authority who will levy or charge rates will assess you, as the occupier of your home, to general rates. These are usually calculated as so many pence to the pound and this figure is the general rate, which may itself be a total of different levies by, for example, a metropolitan authority, a borough and, in some boroughs, the Inner London Education Authority. To calculate the amount of rates which you have to pay you multiply the general rate by the rateable value applying to your home.

It may be that one or more other authorities will assess you to charges based upon the rateable value. One example will be the local water authority which will charge water and sewerage rates which are calculated in much the same way as a general rate.

If you live in a dwelling-house used wholly for the purposes of private dwelling or dwellings then the rate in the pound which is declared by the local authority will be reduced by an amount which is declared from time to time by the Secretary of State. This deduction is known as the 'standard amount' and it is calculated in exactly the same way as the general rate but is a deduction from it.

17.10 Business occupation of your home *(GRA 1967, s. 48)*

If your home is not occupied wholly as a private dwelling, but is a 'mixed hereditament' then you would only be entitled to a proportion of the 'standard amount' of discount which is generally available to domestic property; a mixed hereditament is one where more than one-eighth of the total rateable value is attributable to a part used not for domestic purposes.

It may be difficult to determine whether your home is 'used wholly for the purposes of a private dwelling'. If a garage, outhouse, garden or yard is not used wholly for private dwelling but forms part of it, then that will be ignored in determining whether the whole of your home is a 'private dwelling', so you would enjoy the full standard deduction, even if, for example, you carry on a small metalworking business in your garage.

If one or more rooms in your home are used exclusively for some other purpose (and not used for the purpose even partly of a private dwelling) then to that extent you will not be entitled to the standard amount of reduction for domestic property in calculating your rates.

If substantially the whole of your property is let in rooms singly for residential purposes, then the property will not be treated at all as used for the purposes of a private dwelling.

On the other hand if your home forms part of some larger building which itself is not a dwelling, but which is exempt from rates (such as a church, if you live in a flat over the church hall) then that flat will be rated as if it were a dwelling-house, with the usual standard deduction.

17.11 Alterations to your home *(GRA 1967, s. 6; LGA 1974, s. 21)*

Certain alterations or improvements to your home may give rise to a revision of the rateable value. Amongst the alterations which could give rise to such a revaluation would be:

(a) The addition of central heating or the extension of the central heating system by the addition of further radiators.
(b) The installation of gas heaters.
(c) The installation of electric heaters.
(d) The building of an extension.
(e) The building of a swimming-pool.
(f) The division of the property from a single home to two or more parts each of which is capable of being separately occupied and therefore separately rated, or the merging of two or more parts to make a single home.

Alterations to or the installation of a central heating system or *other* alterations which will not increase the gross value by more than £30 are ignored *if they were made after 1 April 1974.*

17.12 If you make an alteration to your home which reduces its value, you may claim that your 'gross value' should be reduced. Perhaps you demolish a lightly built lean-to extension which is unsatisfactory. If subsequently you construct a new and better conservatory, but the potential increase in the gross value is less than £30, the Valuation Officer cannot seek to increase the value again. If, however, you make alterations to your home (other than the installation or extension of central heating) which, taken together, would increase the gross value by more than £30, then the Valuation Officer may propose an increase in the gross value of your home.

If the Valuation Officer considers that a change to the rateable value of your home is required he may seek information or the right to enter the premises to see what changes have been made.

There is a detailed appeal procedure which may be followed if you are not satisfied with a proposed change to the rateable value of your home.

17.13 How can you ask for your rates to be reduced?

There are a number of circumstances in which you may be able to reduce the rates which you are asked to pay. These are:

(a)   Rate rebate.
(b)   If you suffer from 'temporary disturbance'.
(c)   If your home is occupied as part of a farm.

17.14   Rate rebate   *(LGA 1974, s. 11; s. 12; s. 13; s. 14)*

Rates are not assessed on your ability to pay or on your income but on the property which you occupy. In some circumstances, particularly if you have a low income, this can result in rates being the equivalent of a very high level of tax.

Arrangements have therefore been made to give a rebate or reduction in such circumstances. There are two different schemes for calculating rebates known as the 'statutory rate rebate scheme' and the 'local rate rebate scheme'. You should approach your local authority to find out which of the two schemes will be more advantageous for you. Your local authority may not operate a local rate rebate scheme in which case you are still entitled to the rebates set out under the statutory rate rebate scheme.

You are entitled to a rate rebate, broadly speaking, if you are the person who lives in the premises and pays the rates. If you pay rent to a landlord and your rent is inclusive of rates, you are still entitled to a rate rebate.

The calculation of rate rebates is complex. The calculation takes into account not only your actual income, to which is added notional income (calculated by reference to any capital which you may have), but also your outgoings such as the number of dependants which you have and the amount of the rates themselves.

If you consider that you may be entitled to a rate rebate you should talk to your local authority or Citizens Advice Bureau who will give you guidance.

17.15   Temporary disturbance

If the surroundings of your home are changed by some temporary phenomenon, you may be able to claim that your rates should be reduced whilst you suffer from disturbance. The sort of circumstances which may give rise to such 'temporary disturbance' would be:

(a)   The construction of a road near your home.
(b)   Delay in making up roads on a new housing estate to which you have moved.

(c) Tipping of refuse on adjoining land.
(d) Laying a sewer across your garden.
(e) The use of land near your home for construction work.
(f) The destruction of a hedge which previously gave a high degree of privacy.

If you suffer from one or more such situations you should seek advice from a qualified surveyor experienced in rating questions on the possibility of obtaining a reduction in your rates.

17.16 Agricultural property *(GRA 1967, s. 26(2))*

If your home is an 'agricultural dwelling-house' then its rateable value may be considerably reduced, particularly if your farm is in an area considered as desirable by commuters who seek homes in the country. The reduction arises because in assessing the rateable value, the hypothetical rent calculation explained in 17.7 is made ignoring any potential non-agricultural tenant.

In order to establish that your home ranks for such relief it must be established that it is either a house occupied in connection with agricultural land and used as the dwelling of a person who is primarily engaged in carrying on or directing agricultural operations on that land or, alternatively, that you are employed in agricultural operations on that land in the service of the occupier thereof and are entitled, either as tenant or otherwise, to use the house only whilst so employed.

Note that agricultural dwelling-houses do not have to be situated on the agricultural land but only have to be 'occupied in connection with it'.

If you claim that your house is occupied in connection with agricultural land (other than as an employee) you must show that your are 'primarily' engaged in carrying on or directing agricultural operations. This is a question of fact and will be determined having regard to the amount of time you spend on your farming activities as opposed to other activities, on the money which you earn and whether the farm may be convenient in location to your other activities.

17.17   Letting your property and rates

If you have to let your home, one of the factors which will determine the amount of rent which you charge will be whether you or your tenant is responsible for paying rates. In the case of most furnished tenancies it is the landlord and not the tenant who has to pay rates. If your home is in London, it may be that your tenant will be an ambassador or a member of his staff. In practical terms, ambassadors do not pay rates on properties which they or their staff occupy and you may find that the embassy will arrange that they are responsible for payment of rates on your home (because in practice they will not pay). The rent which you will be able to seek from such a tenant will be accordingly reduced.

18 Some problems and their solutions

18.1 Marriage and two homes

My wife and I were married two years ago and we each had our own flat before our marriage. I had a mortgage of £20,000 and my wife had a mortgage of £25,000 on our respective flats. We decided to move into my wife's flat and sell my flat, but were unable to do so at the right price, and so we let the flat. We now want to move to my original flat and sell my wife's flat. Will we:

(a) get interest relief on the mortgage for my wife's flat whilst we try to sell it?

(b) be able to claim full interest relief on my flat even though there has been a period when it was not occupied as our principal private residence?

Answer The rules for bridging loans explained in 2.9 are extended to cover a case such as yours, at least in part, by extra-statutory concession A38 which is explained in 6.2. For the first 12 months after you left your flat, even if it was empty, you would have been entitled to relief for interest paid on *your* mortgage but only if you had sold it within the period. (It appears that you may not be *entitled* to relief for the period up to when your flat was let, but ask your Inspector of Taxes whether the concession will be extended to you.) Thereafter you can offset mortgage interest against the rental income you received as explained in 7.13.

If you move into your old flat you are entitled to claim relief on interest on *your* mortgage but not on your wife's mortgage. This is because she has owned her flat for more than a year, so you can no longer claim bridging relief. The rules, even with the concession mentioned above, have worked very harshly in your case. You would do better to sell your wife's flat before moving back to yours, as you can claim relief in respect of interest paid on your mortgage while your flat is let and on your wife's mortgage while you both live in her flat. So long as your flat is let the mortgage on it is ignored in establishing whether jointly your mortgages exceed £30,000.

You may be subject to a charge to CGT if you sell your flat before you return to it, or if you sell your wife's flat more than two years after you have vacated it.

18.2 Financing joint improvements

My next-door neighbour and I are both interested in cars and our houses are semi-detached, each with our other neighbour. We want to build a joint garage between our two houses for the cars. My mortgage is £20,000 and my neighbour's £30,000. The garage will cost £3,000 to build and we have agreed to split the repayments on a full borrowing of £3,000 equally. Will we both get interest relief and, if my neighbour will not, can I take out the full borrowing and charge my neighbour a rent equal to his half of the interest?

Answer   You have not said in your question on whose land the joint garage is to be built. The answer assumes that the garage is partly on the land of each of you. Your solicitors should, in any event, be asked to ensure that the deeds to your homes spell out who owns what. If the rateable value of either of your homes is increased by more than £30 you may find your homes' rateable value (and so your rate bill) increases.

Your neighbour already has borrowings of £30,000 so he cannot claim any further mortgage interest relief.

If you and your neighbour each own an interest in the garage, then you can claim relief for whatever proportion of the loan is attributable to the share of the interest you pay (see 2.23). There seems to be no reason why you cannot claim relief for the whole interest if you pay it all. If you charge your neighbour rent for his share then that will be taxable income in your hands. Overall you will, together, be neither better nor worse off than if your neighbour paid his half share of the interest but obtained no tax relief on it.

If your neighbour's interest in cars extends to a trade of repairing or dealing in cars, he could obtain tax relief on the interest he would pay on the garage or on rent he pays you, in both cases as a business expense and not as mortgage interest relief.

18.3   Time sharing

I acquired a time-share flat for four weeks in Scotland for 99 years for £7,000 and borrowed £4,000 to finance this. I do not intend to use the time share for two weeks this year and will rent it out. Will I be able to offset the interest paid against the interest on the borrowed money? Would it make any difference if I let the property for all four weeks?

Answer   As explained in 8.41.1, you cannot obtain relief for interest paid on the acquisition of a time share. Indeed it would appear that even if you purchased 30 weeks of a time share and let the property for 26 weeks or even the whole period, you could not bring the letting within the provisions explained in 7.14.

18.4   MIRAS: delays

I am self-employed and acquired my home last November with a mortgage of £17,500. I completed the MIRAS documentation immediately and sent it to my tax office. When I had not been

advised of a net payment by April I spoke to the tax office and
asked them why my payments were gross. They said that they
had not processed the form and therefore it would only be next
year that my payments would be under MIRAS. This means
that the tax relief will only be given against my tax payable next
January and July and not as my mortgage payments are made. Is
this correct and do I have any redress against them for the extra
cost to me?

Answer   Unfortunately, MIRAS is an administrative procedure and there is nothing you can do to change the situation
except complain. You should write to the District Inspector of
the district which deals with your tax affairs and express your
dissatisfaction. Your loss is a loss only of cash flow but if your
income was small or you suffer a loss for tax purposes from your
business you may have a real loss because you cannot reclaim the
tax which you would have saved under the special MIRAS rules
for low incomes (see 3.14).

18.5   MIRAS and a loan over £30,000

I have a mortgage of £35,000 on my house and understand from
the building society that they will not operate MIRAS on a loan
over £30,000. Can I reduce this borrowing with them to
£30,000 and borrow £5,000 elsewhere and still be able to get
MIRAS relief now without losing any tax relief that might be
available should the £30,000 limit be increased? Would it be
possible, should the limit be increased, to borrow again from the
building society to bring the whole loan within MIRAS?

Answer   There is no reason, in principle, why the building
society should not switch your repayment to MIRAS once the
sum borrowed falls below £30,000; indeed, they *must* then
switch to MIRAS if your home is still your sole or main
residence and not used for some other purpose. What relief you
may be entitled to if there is a further increase in the £30,000
limit must be a question of speculation. When the allowable

limit was raised with effect from 6 April 1983 from £25,000 to £30,000, loans which had been taken out *previously* and which, except for the fact that they exceeded £25,000, qualified for relief, were included in the increased limit. The comments which have been made by the Chancellor of the Exchequer and by the Shadow Chancellor suggest that no change to the limit is likely in the near future.

18.6   Building society loan and deferred interest while unemployed

My building society has written to me saying that, even though I am unemployed and they have agreed to stand over payments on my mortgage for six months or until I find another job, interest will continue to be charged. They also say that no tax relief will be due until I start to make payments again. Is this correct?

Answer   The building society are correct. You are entitled to tax relief when you pay your interest. At present you are not *paying* the building society. If the building society arrange that you pay only the interest element of your repayments, then you would enjoy relief, but if your mortgage is under MIRAS, you will only pay the net interest. It does not appear that you are losing a benefit by not enjoying tax relief now.

18.7   Coding notice

My mortgage is not on MIRAS and the building society statement shows interest charged at 31 December last of £603.62, but my coding notice only shows £550 as allowed. I cannot persuade my tax office to change this. What can I do?

Answer   You have not said for which tax year your coding notice has been issued, but if your building society statement for the year ended 31 December 1983 showed interest paid of £603.52, this figure should not appear on your coding notice for

1984/85. You should ask your building society for a form MIRAS 5 immediately after 5 April 1984, and this will show what interest the building society expects you to pay during the 12 months from 6 April 1984 to 5 April 1985. It is this forecast figure which should agree with the figure in your notice of coding. You might compare your coding notice for the past year (1983/84) with the interest shown as paid in that year on the MIRAS 5. If it differs you should tell your Inspector of Taxes.

18.8   What rate of interest?

My father lent me £10,000 to buy my house and I have paid him interest for the last three years at 10%. He now wants me to have £2,000 of the loan as a gift but to increase the interest rate to 12½% so that his income each year is the same. I am happy to do this if I get interest relief on the full amount. Will this work?

Answer   The only restriction on the *rate* of interest which you may claim as allowable is to be found in FA 1972, s. 75(2), which provides that 'Where interest is paid at a rate in excess of a reasonable commercial rate relief . . . shall not be given in respect of so much of the interest as represents the excess'. On the face of it a rate of 12½% is not in excess of a reasonable commercial rate and so the scheme would be effective.

18.9   Replacing one loan with another and borrowing more at the same time

I have a loan of £3,000 which I borrowed from my own self-employed pension scheme. The rate of interest I pay is linked to bank base rate and I used the money for a loft extension, increasing my total borrowings to £11,500. If I replace this loan by increasing my ordinary mortgage at a lower rate of interest but do not repay my pension scheme and use the new money for a car will I still get tax relief at the higher rate on the interest I pay to my pension scheme fund?

Answer   The answer to your question depends on whether your car is purchased for use in your trade or profession. If you are in non-pensionable employment, the answer to your question is no. As explained in 2.2, the allowability of interest is based on the purpose for which money is borrowed. Although when borrowed, the loan from your self-employed pension scheme was for a qualifying purpose, if you borrow money from your building society it appears that this will not replace your previous borrowing, but will be used to buy a car which is not automatically a 'specified purpose'. If you are self-employed, it may be, however, that the car is being purchased to use in your business or profession, in which case the money is borrowed for a 'specified purpose'. Unfortunately, this would then mean that your building society loan would now not be wholly for the acquisition of your sole or main residence, so strictly speaking, should no longer fall within the MIRAS arrangements. If you use the loan from the building society to repay the loan from your pension fund and then borrow afresh from the pension fund to buy the car, this problem would not arise. You would then enjoy tax relief on all the interest you pay *and* continue to enjoy the cash-flow benefit of MIRAS on your increased building society loan.

18.10   Divorce and two homes

My wife and I are getting divorced and we plan to convert our house into two flats. Our joint mortgage at present is £15,000 and the house is worth £25,000, and we believe each flat would be worth £14,000. I intend to take over the whole mortgage. Will I still get tax relief on the whole loan?

Answer   You would get tax relief on the whole loan — see Chapter 6. It is not clear whether each of you will own one flat. If so, will the mortgage be divided? A half attributable to each flat? How are you going to take over the whole mortgage? Are you going to pay the building society directly on a joint mortgage or pay your wife's mortgage payments or pay her maintenance from which she will pay her mortgage payments? Whichever method is used you will effectively enjoy tax relief on the whole loan.

18.11 Money borrowed to buy out an existing tenant

We have been abroad for six years and have let our unmortgaged home for most of the time. We intend to return next year but the current tenants have a lease for another two years. We intend to rent somewhere in the meantime. Can we get any tax relief on the rent we will be paying? If not, could we take out a mortgage to pay off our tenants and claim tax relief on the mortgage?

Answer   There is no provision under which you could claim tax relief for rent which you might pay if you live somewhere while your home is let. If you borrowed money to buy out the tenants' interest in your home so that you could move back there, you can obtain tax relief on the interest you pay, but not on the purchase itself. It is doubtful whether the cost of buying out your tenants, whose lease will have expired in two years, would be treated as an allowable expense in calculating the gain you might make (if you are chargeable to CGT when you sell your house) because the interests of the tenants would have expired at the date of sale (if made more than two years from now) (see 8.18).

18.12   Sale of part of a house by instalments

My basement is let to students who now want to buy the flat from me for £15,000. They cannot afford to pay immediately but want to pay off £5,000 a year and pay rent on the balance outstanding to the equivalent rate to the full rent. How will I be taxed on the rent and will I be making gains of £5,000 in three different years?

Answer   Firstly, if you are selling your basement for £15,000, that does not mean that you have a chargeable gain of £15,000. The basement forms part of a larger house which you must have acquired at some cost. You may deduct a fair proportion of the cost from the proceeds. Secondly, unless the basement is completely cut off from the rest of the house and you have not lived in the house as your home at all, you may be entitled to the special relief for gains of up to £20,000, explained in 8.33. Thirdly, if you sell now to the students, are you selling a one-third part of the basement each year or are you selling the whole basement on deferred terms? If the former then you will be making a gain each year, but only on the basis of selling a one-third share of your basement — broadly, you might expect one-third of the full gain to arise in each year. On the figures you have given, and if you have no other chargeable gains in the year, you would have no CGT to pay. The rent payable in respect of the unsold fraction of the basement would continue to be taxable in the same way as the rent you receive now.

It does seem, however, rather a laborious procedure. On the figures you give it might save considerable legal fees if you sell the basement subject to a charge on it for unpaid instalments, particularly if you may claim £20,000 exemption from CGT so that the whole disposal proceeds are free of CGT even if all treated as receivable in one year. Instead of rent you would collect interest on the unpaid instalments.

18.13   Conversion of a house into flats and their disposal

My husband died five years ago and left me the house we lived in, which was too big for me. My son has converted the house into 3 flats and he is going to live in one and I will live in another. I want my son to have his flat for the work done and we will sell the other flat. A friend has told me that I will have to pay tax on the sale of the flat. Is this correct and do I have any other taxes to pay?

Answer You are proposing to dispose of two flats: one by way of a gift to your son and the other by way of a sale. You have not given any idea of the values concerned so the answer will have to be on the basis of assumed figures.

Suppose when your husband died the house was worth £40,000. Your son has *spent* on the conversion, say, £14,000. The conversion took him, say, 18 months. Each flat is worth, say, £24,000 now.

Firstly, there will be no charge to CGT on either disposal since the house was, within the last two years, your principal private residence (see 8.9).

Secondly, there may be an event for CTT (see 9.1) when you transfer the flat to your son although probably no tax would actually be payable.

You would be giving the flat to your son when it was worth £24,000, but he has spent £14,000 on the conversion. You would be treated as having made a gift to him of £24,000 – £14,000, i.e., £10,000. It is assumed that the two flats remaining are still worth £48,000, so that the value of what your son receives is equal to your loss of wealth.

If, in the fiscal year you give the flat and in the previous year you have made no CTT gifts, then £6,000 out of the £10,000 gift will be exempt. You will have made a chargeable gift of £4,000 which will be treated as part of the £64,000 of gifts which are taxed at a nil rate.

18.14 A home provided by your employer and an option to purchase it

Four years ago I was headhunted by a large multinational, which company purchased a house in London for £100,000 and allowed me to live there for payment of rent equivalent to the rateable value. After two years, i.e., some 20 months ago, I took out an option to purchase the house for £110,000 on payment of £1,000 to my employer. At the same time I agreed with them that I could subdivide the house and sublet it as I wanted. This resulted in the house being converted into two flats one of which has been sublet as a self-contained unit. The tenant now wishes to buy the flat he is in for £75,000 (the one I live in being worth the same). The costs of conversion were £15,000, which I funded by way of a bank loan. How much tax would I have to pay if I exercised the option and sold the flat occupied by the tenant to him, funding the whole purchase by way of a loan from my employer?

Answer

(a) It would seem that for the tax year 1984/85 you would be taxable on the benefit of the home provided by your employer (assuming it is not representative occupation), calculated as follows:

	£
Rateable value, less rent paid (= rateable value)	nil
12% × (£100,000 − £75,000)	3,000
	3,000

(b) You may be taxable further if the District Valuer is of the view that when the option to purchase at £110,000 was granted for a consideration of £1,000, the option was worth more than £1,000 in the open market. Such an undervaluation would be itself treated as a Schedule E benefit and so chargeable to income tax.

(c) As you refer to the flat having a subtenant, you presumably receive the rent from the subtenant; so you must pay income tax on this rent. It does not appear that you can claim to offset the notional interest on which you are taxed, i.e., the £3,000 p.a. mentioned in (a).

(d) Until you exercise your option, you do not own an interest *in* land; you have not expended the money borrowed from the bank on improving *your* land, but that of your

employer. It seems that in these circumstances you would
have no right to claim income tax relief on the interest you
pay to the bank. On a strict reading of the law, even after
you exercise your option, you would not be entitled to
claim tax relief on the interest you pay to the bank, because
you did not borrow that money for a 'specified purpose'
(see 2.2).

(e)   (i)   If you exercise your option and pay your employer
              £110,000, then you may have to pay capital gains tax
              on the profit you make, because the purchase was
              partly for the purpose of realising a gain from
              disposing of the flat to your tenant (see 8.44).

The tax would be calculated as follows:

	£
Cost of house	110,000
Cost of option	1,000
Cost of conversion	15,000
	£126,000

$$\frac{\text{Cost of portion}}{\text{sold}} = \frac{\text{value of portion sold}}{\text{value of whole}} \times \frac{\text{cost of}}{\text{whole}}$$

$$= \frac{£75,000}{£75,000 + £75,000} \times £126,000 \qquad = 63,000$$

Sale proceeds   = 75,000

Profit   12,000*

*Chargeable to capital gains tax but see (e)(ii)
below.

Although you have owned the option to acquire
your home for less than two years, you cannot claim
the exemption explained in 8.9. You have not

owned an interest *in* your home before you exercise your option.

(ii) There is a possibility that you might be charged to income tax, and not to CGT, on the gain by virtue of the anti-avoidance provisions of ICTA, s. 488. This provides that where land or an interest in land is acquired with the sole or main object of realising a gain of a capital nature, the gain may be charged not to CGT but to income tax under Schedule D Case VI. The elaborate rules which deal with this situation are not applied if, when acquired, the property was your sole or main home even if it was acquired to be resold at a profit. The date of acquisition is only when you exercise your option; at that date the flat you are selling was tenanted (and so not your sole or main residence).

(f) The loan from your employer would itself be treated as a taxable benefit, and you would be taxed on the benefit based on an assumed rate of interest of 12% on the whole loan (less any interest you pay to your employer).

18.15 Overseas employment and two homes

In 1976 I was posted abroad by my employers. I let my home in England, which I had purchased in 1974 for £30,000, and it has remained tenanted ever since. In 1983, while still abroad, I purchased another house in England which I intended to occupy when I return to England in 1987. When I come back I expect to sell my original home which is now worth £100,000. Do I have any tax to pay when I sell?

Answer If you sell your original home before you return to England, then the sale will be at a time you are not resident in the UK and so not chargeable (in the UK) to CGT. You should check that you would not be chargeable to tax wherever you then live in respect of such a sale. If you sell while you are non-resident the special withholding provisions for DLT (see 11.18) will not be applied to you if the house is worth not more than £150,000 when your sell.

If you wait to sell your original home until you return, you will enjoy exemption from CGT on the sale *only if* you return *in fact* (if only for a very short time) to your original home before selling it (see 8.21). The exemption will not apply if you do not return to your original home because the three-year period mentioned in 8.23 has been exceeded.

If you return to Britain and move directly to your new home and then sell your original home, you would be chargeable to CGT on a proportion of the gain calculated as follows (ignoring indexation allowance):

	£
Proceeds of sale	100,000
Cost	30,000
Gain	70,000

Exempt period 1974 to 1976 (principal private residence)	2 years
Chargeable 1976 to 1987	12 years
Total period of ownership	14 years

Chargeable to CGT: $\dfrac{12 \text{ years}}{14 \text{ years}} \times £70,000 = £60,000$

Note that you cannot claim that the last two years before sale are exempt because you do not fall within the exemption explained in 8.9.

Appendix

Comparison between capital gains tax and interest relief on your home

	Interest relief	Capital gains tax
1. Definition of 'sole or main residence'	Question of fact only	If more than one property your option to claim which one
2. Temporary absence when not in job-related accommodation	Minimal relief	Extensive reliefs, minimum two years, no overall maximum
3. Territorial limits	For interest relief property must be within the UK or the Republic of Ireland	No territorial limits
4. Maximum amount on which claim may be made	Loans totalling no more than £30,000	No limit
5a. Dependent relative	No limit to number of dependent relatives but aggregate mortgages must not exceed £30,000	No financial limit but only one dependent relative per married couple

	Interest relief	Capital gains tax
5b. On death of dependent relative	Relief stops at date of death	Two-year period after date of death during which exemption continues
6. Property let for part of a period	Interest either wholly allowable or wholly not allowable	Let period partly ignored. Balance restricts exempt amount on pro rata basis
7. Divorce and separation	Relief potentially starts from date of separation	Exemption ends from end of year of assessment in which separation takes place but parties still 'connected' until divorce
8. Working from home — effect on tax liability	Actual use may give relief	Exclusive use may restrict relief

Glossary

There are a number of words or phrases used throughout this book which have a special or technical meaning. The words and phrases used are as follows:

Basic-rate tax. The rate of income tax applied to all incomes subject to income tax: at present 30%. This is equivalent to 3/7ths of the 'net of income tax' payments made. If basic-rate tax is deducted before you receive income the amount you actually receive is 'net' (see 'Gross payments'). See also 'Higher-rate tax'.

Benefit. If you receive any advantage from your employment, which is not in money but is in money's worth, it will be a *benefit* and may be subject to income tax in your hands.

Capital allowances. If, in connection with your trade or profession, you buy 'plant or machinery' then a special allowance will be given to you as a deduction from your income for income tax purposes. Except in the case of motor cars and certain expenses in connection with farms, relief was 100% of the sum expended if before 14 March 1984. Subsequently, the relief was 75% for expenditure up to 31 March 1985 and 50% for expenditure from 1 April 1985 to 31 March 1986. The balance of the expenditure is relieved for tax at 25% of the previously unrelieved balance each year.

Dependent relative. This term is used in a special sense for the purposes of capital gains tax and interest relief (see 2.12). This is *not* the definition used in income tax law for personal allowances given when you support an elderly relative.

Employer. Where *benefits* are in question, an employer is any person who actually employs you, *or any other person* who provides a *benefit* because of your employment.

Fiscal year. The 12 months commencing on 6 April in one calendar year and ending on 5 April in the following calendar year. See also 'Year of assessment'.

Gross payment. Where the payer of interest is bound by law to deduct tax (or, as in the case of a building society and, after 5 April 1985, a bank, is deemed to have done so) before paying the interest to you, then the gross payment is:

$$\frac{10}{7} \times \text{sum you receive}$$

Home. Where you live — this can be a house, a flat, a caravan or a houseboat. The rules for tax relief are the same, whether you own all or part of, or an interest in, your home.

Higher-rate tax. For taxable incomes in excess of £15,400 the rate of tax applicable for individuals is more than 30%, as explained in 1.8. The extra tax will be collected separately if the income has already suffered basic-rate tax.

Job-related accommodation. If your employer provides a home for you then such a home may be job-related accommodation (see 2.17). Your occupation of such a home is called 'representative occupation' (see 10.8). Similar circumstances may arise if you are self-employed and in that connection your home is provided by somebody else (see 16.17).

MIRAS. Mortgage interest relief at source (see Chapter 3).

Mortgage. Money borrowed *on security* of a property — the lender is the 'mortgagee' and the borrower is the 'mortgagor'. The mortgage is a charge on the property, and usually the lender will hold the documents of title. A second mortgage is money borrowed on security of the property where there is already a mortgage which is not repaid. As a mortgagee who has the first charge holds the title deeds, the lender who provides the second mortgage can only secure himself by registering a land charge.

If you borrow money to help you purchase your home and the lender does not ask for a charge on it, then the money you have borrowed is not a mortgage, but the interest may still rank for tax relief (see 2.3).

Personal allowances. Deductions from taxable income allowed (see 1.8) to individuals resident in the United Kingdom and to certain other individuals in part (see 12.13).

Personal representatives. The person or persons who, on a death, is or are legally entitled to deal with the affairs of the deceased. If you make a will, when it has been proved, the persons named and acting as your executors will be your personal representatives. If you do not make a will, or for some reason your will is ineffective so that you die 'intestate', individuals who may have an interest under the laws of intestacy may apply to the Probate Court for a grant of administration so that they may be appointed your 'personal representatives'. In such a case they must obey the strict rules setting out who may inherit whatever wealth you may have left.

Year of assessment. The period for which your income is calculated for the purpose of assessment to income tax or capital gains tax. The period is described by reference to the calendar years which it spans so that the year of assessment 1984/85 is the period from 6 April 1984 to 5 April 1985. If you are only chargeable to tax for a part of a fiscal year, the year of assessment will be the whole of that fiscal year.

Index

The following abbreviations have been used in subdivisions in this index: CGT = Capital gains tax; CTT = Capital transfer tax; DLT = Development land tax; VAT = Value added tax.

Husbands *see* Spouses
Income
    definition   2
    from abroad   3
    from an employer   3
    from sources outside UK   5
    from trade/profession   3
Income tax   2–3
    allowances   6–8
    and 'hobby farming'   204–5
    basic rate, definition   233
    coding notices   221–2
    collection   4
    deduction by employer   4
    form 930   4
    higher rate   235
    on benefits   234
    on home provided by employer
        137
    scale   5
    Schedule A   2
        furnished lettings   77, 78
        unfurnished lettings   80–2
    Schedule B   2–3
    Schedule C   3
    Schedule D   3
        furnished lettings   77, 78, 82–4
    Schedule E   3
    Schedule F   3
    working from home   197–8
    year of assessment, definition 235
Indexation relief on sale of home
    109–12
Individuals, defined   2
Infants, gifts to, and income tax 8
Insurance companies
    home loans   51–3
    'top-up' mortgages   53
Interest on home loans   3, 8,
    14–29, 217–18
    compared with CGT relief
        22, 231–2
    gross payment   234
    in respect of lettings   86
    on coding notices   221–2
    on mortgage on overseas home
        168–9
    paid to vendors   59–60
    paid while unemployed   221
    payable after death   28
    when employer requires a move
        elsewhere   165

Job-related accommodation 23–4, 25
    and CGT on second home 115–16
    and MIRAS   40
    and second homes   26
    definition   234
    option to purchase   226–8
Jointly owned property, valuation
    for CTT   131
Land
    change of use   148
    current use value   150–1
    inherited, DLT and CTT
        implications   153–4
    loans for acquisition   15
    realised development value 147–8
        definition   148–9
    relevant base value, calculation 149
    stamp duty on sale   183–4
        see also Development land tax
Lettings   72–90
    and interest relief   86
    as income from a trade   85
    borrowing to buy out tenant 224
    by husband and wife, with
        husband abroad   162–4
    effect on CGT upon sale of
        home   105–9
    furnished   77
        allowable costs   78
        Schedule A or D, factors
            influencing   78
        Schedule D   82–4
    general outgoings   72–4
    in shared accommodation 76–7
    losses   82, 85
    rates   216
    shared accommodation   75–6
    unfurnished, Schedule A   80–2
    when not resident in UK 159–61
    wife as housekeeper   75–6
        see also Holiday homes; Rents
Life insurance policies, and
    CGT   10
Loans for home purchase/
    improvement   14–15, 178
    amount of tax relief   17–18
    and job-related accommodation
        23–4
    and year in which you marry
        61–2
    effect of previous borrowings
        for other purposes   20
    for second homes   24, 26